PRODUCTIVITY FOR SCHOOL BUSINESS PROFESSIONALS

JULIE CORDINER

SCHOOL FINANCIAL SUCCESS PUBLICATIONS

Productivity for School Business Professionals

Published by School Financial Success Publications

https://schoolfinancialsuccess.com

Cover design: JD Smith

ISBN: 978-0-9955902-3-6

*For all school business professionals,
who do such an amazing job.*

CONTENTS

PART I

PART II

PART III

PART I

INTRODUCTION

This book provides a pathway to improved productivity for School Business Professionals, helping you maximise your personal and professional effectiveness through self-care and a strong focus on what matters most.

You'll find a host of tips, techniques and practical activities to help you manage your time, beat procrastination and create productive habits. A companion workbook is also available for you to record your progress and be reflective as you complete the activities.

Invest in yourself and reap the rewards.

1

THE PRODUCTIVITY TRAIL

What is productivity?

The concept of productivity began in production industries, but it has become a personal attribute we are expected to aim for. I like to think of productivity as our individual impact: how we make our time count and produce our best work in the areas that matter most to us. If we get it right, we can achieve our goals with less effort and fewer distractions.

You may have a different definition, and that's absolutely fine. The important thing is that by choosing to read this book, you've already decided you want to improve.

In many circles, productivity is defined as getting more done. But that's not helpful; it implies we should accept ever-increasing demands. The hamster-wheel mentality isn't doing us any favours. When we're exhausted, we fall off, and it takes a lot of effort to get back on again.

There are many uncertainties in this world, and many things we can't control. It's better not to worry unduly about events until they happen; I prefer to do just enough thinking to ensure I'm in a state of readiness when decisions are taken.

But there are three important things that you <u>can</u> control:

1 - What is important to you;

2 - What you focus on;

3 - What you do to create the results you want.

To be more productive, you need to decide what matters most to you and focus your best energy on that. I also believe everyone's number one goal should be self-care. To create the results you want, you need to be physically strong and mentally resilient.

Similarly, three factors will determine how you handle excessive demands: your mindset, what you choose to work on and how you organise your time to complete it. Do you have unrealistic expectations of yourself, demanding far more of yourself than anyone else would? Are you too ready to accept more work without stopping to consider whether it is essential for you to do it, or whether someone else could?

In this book, I will show you how to challenge your own thinking and practices, so you can find a better balance. Whether you are an experienced SBP looking to tweak your existing practice, or relatively new to the role, you will find a wide range of ideas, tips and techniques to try out. I'll help you find your own path to maximise your personal and professional effectiveness.

The root of the problem

Society is changing and so is the way we work. Technology has brought significant benefits, removing drudgery, automating many tasks, and creating new types of jobs. It has helped us to be more efficient and enabled innovative solutions, but it has also placed increasing demands on us. Experts believe the pace of technological change will be even faster in the future.

We have numerous tools at our disposal to keep in touch with others, but if we're not careful, they can monopolise our time and create unhelpful habits. It's hard to separate work from the rest of our life, from emails on our phones to social media being used for multiple purposes. No wonder we feel our time is not our own, as everyone competes for our attention.

Our ability to access information has been transformed in ways we could only dream of twenty years ago, but the downside is that we have much greater expectations of each other. When we pose a question or ask for help, we assume we'll get an answer straight away. There seems to be no end to the demands placed on us.

It's easy to believe you'll never achieve anything. You feel you're not in control, that you're at the beck and call of other people, dancing to their tune and responding to their priorities instead of your own. A lack of control is known to be a major cause of stress.

Issues specific to education

Delegated responsibilities weigh much more heavily on school leaders than they used to, not only because funding hasn't kept pace with cost pressures in recent years, but also because the sources of support have been considerably weakened. Schools have had to plug gaps in services but haven't received any additional funding. The core budget therefore gets squeezed more and more.

It's not only about the amount of money available; it's also what you're expected to achieve with it. With every annual set of test and exam results, there is increasing pressure to perform. The Ofsted framework and national curriculum keep changing, and the high-stakes accountability system makes it hard to compromise on the quality of provision.

Consequently, there is a constant battle to balance pupils' needs with affordability, as you strive to make sure each generation receives an entitlement to an excellent education.

People attracted to a career in schools are usually passionate about their work and committed to doing their absolute best for the children, so they accept the extra responsibilities. But while you can absorb additional pressures for a while, there's a tipping point beyond which it becomes too onerous and can even pose a risk to your health and well-being.

The challenges for SBPs

The role of the school business professional (SBP) is especially vulnerable to overload. I'm using the term SBP to cover all the different job titles that exist.

The idea for this book came as I noticed an increasing number of SBPs reaching out for help on Twitter, showing signs of being overwhelmed. They were unable to see the light at the end of the tunnel, and even if there was one, it was probably an oncoming train.

Financial pressures are causing a real headache and financial forward planning is difficult. The redistribution of funding through the National Funding Formula has helped some schools and disadvantaged others, but the level of historic deficits suggests the difficulties will continue, especially as there is no funding for the 2020 teachers' pay award and (as usual) none for the NJC support staff award.

This sense of overwhelm is understandable in such a broad role. You could be covering all business functions alone, or managing staff in disciplines outside of your experience. Perhaps you are in a single school, or working across multiple schools or academies in a trust. Everyone expects you to provide answers, because you deliver, have a wide-ranging knowledge and a long list of useful contacts, and you are a pragmatic problem solver.

As a result, you are in firefighting mode, on constant alert for the next emergency. You spend most of your time responding to other people's priorities and never your own, plagued by interruptions throughout the day and trying to catch up after office hours. You go to bed with worries tumbling around in your brain, so you don't sleep well, and when you wake up you're not refreshed or ready to join the fray again.

Is this sounding familiar? These are the problems I want to help you resolve.

Another way

The good news is that you don't have to feel overwhelmed forever. While the demands on you probably won't reduce, you can change the way you respond to them. This means changing your mindset and adapting your working practices to prioritise the most important aspects of your role. I'll show you how to tackle both of these key areas, so you can make your own choices.

At the heart of improving your productivity is the need to practise self-care. By taking greater care of yourself, you can do more at work and have the time and energy to enjoy your life outside of it. Over the course of my career, I've realised that paying attention to your own health and well-being is the most important thing you can do. But I've had many false starts along the way. I want to share what I've learned, so you can benefit from it sooner.

Clarity on what you want to achieve in every aspect of your life will help. But to reach your goals, you also need energy, motivation, resilience and thinking space. Being intentional about looking after yourself will make the single biggest difference to each of those.

Context matters

In this book, you will find a range of strategies to increase your productivity and achieve the most important things. But be aware that not all of them will be applicable to your situation.

However, if you get the balance right, you'll have more time for the things that matter most to you, including a more fulfilling life outside of work. It's got to be worth a try, hasn't it?

What makes me able to advise on productivity?

Experience helps us to analyse what works, and that comes with age, so I'm pretty well qualified! Since starting my career in education in 1983, I've seen many changes in policy, funding, structures and services, and have worked with schools of all types in every sector.

Having advised many SBPs, I can see where productivity techniques are well suited to the role. I'm also a governor at a secondary school due to become an academy.

Having spent ten years as an Assistant Director of Education with a very broad remit, I understand what it's like to have responsibility for some areas in which you don't have experience or qualifications, and to spin multiple plates. I have learned a lot about myself; sometimes I've struggled to keep my balance, but have learned how to reset it.

I hope my suggestions will help you choose your own path to a more productive and less stressful life. But above all, I want to emphasise the importance of finding your own way; you are unique, and you need to decide what works for you personally.

Key points

- Productivity is about how we make our time count and produce our best work in the areas which matter most.
- A lack of control is stressful, so tackle the three big things you can control: What is important to you, what you focus on and what you do to create the results you want.
- You can change your mindset and your practices for a better balance.
- Schools are being expected to do more with insufficient funding, but you can only absorb so much extra work before reaching a tipping point, where you are risking your health and well-being.
- Productivity is challenging for SBPs because of the breadth of the role; this book will suggest techniques and tools to help relieve the pressure.
- Self-care is the foundation of a more productive and satisfying life. It will help you be clear about what you want and give you the motivation and energy to go after it.
- Remember that context matters. You are unique, and you need to find the productivity approach that suits you best.

A SYSTEM FOR CHANGE

A tiered approach

We'll be discussing a wide range of approaches to personal and professional effectiveness, but you can decide which to focus on and how you approach them. If you are an experienced SBP, you may only need a refresher in some areas, or a few tweaks to your existing frameworks. If you are relatively new to the role, you have a wonderful chance to set firm foundations for a sustainable approach to your career.

My approach is structured in tiers, starting at the bottom with a foundation of internal needs linked to your mindset and self-care. The next stage comprises the building blocks of organisation, followed by tactics that maximise your productivity. The top layer is where you take action to make it happen. I call it a Productivity Pyramid.

Take
action

Maximise

Organise

Set the foundations

Set the foundations

- Mindset: why it matters. Control your response to situations, avoid self-sabotage, and learn to cope better when things go wrong or in a crisis.
- Self-care: look after yourself in every area of health, find your community for support and learn to relax. Note: I'm not a medical practitioner; you must get expert help if needed.
- Know yourself: listen to your inner voice, follow your beliefs and values, and know what energises or drains you.
- Habits: recognise positive and negative habits, know why they arise, and change yours for better productivity.

Organise

- Goal setting: the power of goals, your definition of success, setting your strategic goals and prioritising them.
- From goals to a plan: break down your goals by importance and schedule your tasks. Know what to change and how to measure your success.
- Be organised: identify your commitments to get the important things done. Learn how to free up brain power, time and energy.

- Set boundaries: why you need them, how to say no, delay, delegate and eliminate tasks and manage expectations.
- Time management: track and analyse how you spend your time, minimise interruptions and master your emails.

Maximise

- Achieve flow: set the conditions for a 'flow state' to achieve focused work. Plan your day, create downtime and make room for relaxation.
- Tackle resistance: what is it, why do we procrastinate, and how can we take action instead?
- Build capacity: business planning, solving underlying problems, balancing reward and effort, hidden talents, self-service and leading change.
- Hone your skills: assess and improve your skills then take action. Convey information well, and be proactive in leadership to avoid conflict.

Take action

- The culture around you: does it match your beliefs and values? Challenge and change it, or decide to move?
- Go steadily, make incremental changes and check what's working before trying other approaches.
- Reflections: a recap on what we've covered.

Take small steps

We fall into habits relatively easily, often without realising, but they can be difficult to change. So don't be over-ambitious when trying to tackle ingrained practices. Identify the biggest obstacles to your effectiveness, and address those first.

Your best chance of success is to take small steps, working on one area at a time and making incremental changes. Consider how the

British Cycling team prepared for the 2012 Olympic Games. Every single element of the bikes, all aspects of each rider's physical and mental state and the psychological approach to the races were examined in minute detail and improved individually before putting it all together to create the optimal combination. As a result, the team achieved tremendous success, far surpassing previous results.

There isn't a 'one size fits all' solution which will magically transform productivity. Everyone is different. The SBP family in England works in over 24,000 schools, all with their own culture and approaches. It's not only how you perform tasks or what systems you use; how you relate to other people plays a big part. Two people can do the same job in similar schools, with different colleagues, and a solution that's right for one won't necessarily work for the other.

I hope you'll find this book offers food for thought. It's always worth trying a range of approaches; you might be surprised at what does or doesn't work. Don't be downhearted if something isn't right for you. Learn from it.

The importance of self-care

While I was writing this book, the theme of self-care kept floating to the top. I make no apologies for the way it pops up everywhere. Looking after yourself makes it easier to keep your purpose in mind, analyse problems and find solutions. If you're exhausted, frazzled, confused or panicked, you won't perform at your best. Prioritising your own health and personal needs can be difficult if you're used to helping everyone else first, but it's crucial.

Since becoming an author, I've been paying attention to creative people, and some of the tips and techniques I advocate come from this background. Don't be put off by this; the principles are universal. Creativity produces ideas, so it's especially valuable when you're searching for solutions. But please note that I'm not talking about creative (as in illegal) accounting!

The need to exercise self-care applies to your approach in trying out the tips and techniques in this book, too. Don't make things harder for yourself by attempting lots of changes at once. Try one thing and give it a while to bed in. Once it's working, you can test out something else. If you've done your best but you can't see a positive impact in a reasonable timescale, ditch it and choose another approach. It's not failure; it's 'test and learn'.

Using the book

You're welcome to use this book as a pick and mix guide or a check-list. Please don't think you have to try everything; you'll be over-whelmed, which will defeat the object altogether! I imagine you won't need every piece of advice; it may be a case of sharpening up some areas and only going deep on a few. Don't try to fix something if it isn't broken. It might simply need a tweak for maximum effect.

For those of you who manage teams, consider using some of the techniques to help your colleagues. This can multiply your effective-ness, because those around you will be improving their own produc-tivity (in their own way, of course) and the things they do to support you will run more smoothly.

I recommend that you do the first activity at the end of this section before reading on. After that, it's up to you whether you (a) do a straight read through to get an overall feel for the content before homing in on the areas you're most interested in exploring, (b) start at the beginning and work through it in order, or (c) go straight to the areas you want to improve most.

The sub-headings within chapters should make it easy to dip in and out. Decide which topics could make the biggest difference to your productivity and focus on those.

I've shown references like this: (link). If you're reading the paper-back, you can go to https://schoolfinancialsuccess.com/psbp-links for a full list of clickable links. If you have the e-book, you'll find some links go straight to articles and resources, but those related to books or products send you to the psbp-links page. Including links to a certain online retailer is frowned upon in a book which is also published on other platforms.

You might feel yourself resisting a particular approach. If so, remember that true learning often happens outside of your comfort zone. Keep an open mind on why you're reluctant and give it a fair chance. It could be a lack of familiarity, or doubts about whether it will work for you. Perhaps you lack confidence in your ability to change. This is only your perception; you might be wrong (I sometimes adopt a 'tough love' approach)! If you dismiss it out of hand, you might miss an opportunity to improve an aspect of your practice.

Self-awareness is important: pay attention to what is becoming easier or more effective and it will motivate you to tackle other areas until you get the right balance for you. Learn to be your own cheerleader.

Many of the activities involve writing about your thoughts and reflecting on them. I encourage you to write by hand; it can bring a deeper creative response, helping us connect with the words and access our subconscious, which is incredibly powerful. I have my best ideas when writing on paper.

An article by Oxford Learning (link) summarises the benefits of writing by hand:

- Stress relief, improving focus and attention;
- Creativity and learning, deepening thinking when done frequently;
- Increased memory and retention, involving more senses and motor neuron activity than typing;
- Improved mood, through writing about feelings, making burdens lighter;
- Better sleep, by writing about gratitude before bedtime.

The Companion Workbook

I've created a printed workbook as a journal for your improvement journey. It contains all the activities in this book, with extra prompts and space to record your responses. If you didn't order it initially, do have a look. It will encourage you to explore your thinking and be reflective as you test out various approaches. Having all your findings in one place will also make it easier to see how far you've progressed.

Before you embark on your journey, record your starting point as a baseline for measuring improvement. Doing the first activity below before reading further in the book will ensure your ideas for change aren't influenced by my suggestions.

Activity 1 - Your starting point

1.1 Find a quiet time and place. Write in your workbook about the position you are starting from. Express your feelings about the situation you're in and the way you approach your work and your personal life.
For it to be helpful as a baseline, be honest, go deep, and recognise the positive and negative aspects. Try to identify the big things you'd like to change. It needs to be personal to you. The workbook contains some prompts to help.
1.2 Reflect on what you've written (after an interval if you can) and add any new thoughts that have occurred to you.

Activity 2 - Time tracking

2.1. Download a time tracking spreadsheet template from the links webpage at https://schoolfinancialsuccess.com/psbp-links.
2.2. Choose a fairly typical week (I know there's no such thing, but just pick one). At regular intervals, record your activity in the relevant time blocks in your worksheet. Create bigger blocks if needed using the Merge Cells function. Try to record a full week; mixing days from different weeks won't give you a complete picture. If you can do two weeks, copy the sheet to a new tab.

2.3. Add useful notes (either on the sheet or in your workbook) about things that weren't typical, any specific challenges, deadlines you were working to, or any other information which will be helpful when you look back at it.

Tips for completing the activity can be found in the first worksheet in the file.

Once you've completed it, put it away for safe keeping. We will be coming back to it later; don't try to analyse the results now.

Key points

- The four steps to better productivity are Set the foundations, Organise, Maximise and Take action.
- Don't try to change too many things at once. Start small, build up layers of improvement and do what works for you.
- Use the companion workbook as a journal to record your starting point and your findings from the activities.

PART II

SET THE FOUNDATIONS

Set the foundations

We're starting at the bottom of our pyramid, laying the foundations for our improvement journey. This part is about setting the right internal conditions to help you maximise your productivity.

If you get this right, it will be much easier to build on it and tackle the other layers, because you will have more resilience. You will also have a useful alert system in place, helping you to recognise and resolve problems at an earlier stage.

You may have your own approach to the areas we'll be discussing, and if it works for you, that's fantastic. This part can be a refresher, a checklist to make sure you are in tip-top condition mentally and physically.

In this part we'll be covering mindset, self-care, knowing yourself, and habits. Let's get going!

3

MINDSET

Why mindset matters

Mindset is your internal belief system, and it plays a big part in the habits you develop. It's worth paying attention to it, because once you become more aware of how you think, you can address the internal barriers which are stopping you from being productive. They can include self-sabotage and ingrained habits which are misdirecting your energies.

We develop routines, sometimes unwittingly, without realising some of them are detrimental to our productivity. It can be hard to accept that the beliefs and perceptions which we have cultivated all our lives are holding us back.

Take a moment to stop and think. Are you subconsciously sending unhelpful messages to yourself, and are they causing you stress? From years of working with SBPs, other school leaders and local authority officers, I've identified some common assumptions which can be toxic if taken too far. I'm also guilty of some of these:

- You are the only person who can do x, y, z;
- You're there to serve others first, every time;

- Working long hours is a badge of honour;
- You can't be seen to fail;
- Perfection matters.

There are many things we can't control in life, but one thing we can learn to control is the way we think.

If we're struggling to complete everything, we might blame the mountain of tasks, or those who have asked us to do them. But are we thinking rationally? Are we accepting duties which others could and should do? Do we try to solve everyone else's problems instead of showing them how to do it themselves? Is perfectionism making us spend far too long on a task for little extra benefit?

There's a movement called Slow Living (link), which challenges our tendency to rush around trying to do everything. It is about being purposeful and finding fulfilment in connecting with yourself, other people and the world around you. Slow Living reduces stress, helping us make calm, conscious decisions about what we do with our time. As with all of my suggestions in this book, you can pick and choose the elements you would like to try.

Controlling your response to a situation

I'm a fan of The Sumo Guy, Paul McGee, after hearing him speak over a decade ago. SUMO (link) stands for either 'Shut Up, Move On' or 'Stop, Understand, Move On', depending on the context. His motivational talks for schools and other organisations provide tips on developing resilience and confidence. The lesson I learned was how to keep things in perspective and control my response to situations.

He talks about 'hippo time', an initial period when you can wallow in misery about whatever's bothering you. But keep it short to avoid being drawn into despair. Avoid the 'Awfulisers', he says, the people who relish painting a gloomy picture. Do you know any? Their excessive sympathy makes you feel worse. Pick yourself up and do something else or find a way to resolve the problem.

Paul also tells us not to wear the victim t-shirt. We shouldn't blame others for our reactions to events; we should try to work out why we respond in a particular way. Then we can take responsibility for our lives, stop the negative thinking and move on.

SUMO is about controlling your reactions to difficult or unpleasant situations. Taking a fresh perspective will help you choose a better path which leads to success. For example, the Covid-19 crisis has been challenging, but has it brought any benefits? Have you found a new, more efficient way to do some aspects of your work?

The SUMO website has some useful downloads (link). I really like the '7 cartoons', which are very pertinent to our mindset topic.

One of my favourite sayings, attributed to Henry Ford, is *'Whether you think you can or think you can't, you're right.'*

Self-belief makes a huge difference to your chances of success. People who think they can't do something probably won't even bother trying, while those who believe they can are more likely to succeed, because they will persist until they achieve their aim. You not only need to have an eye on your goal, but also the conviction that you can reach it.

Don't compartmentalise work and home; both aspects need energy and a problem in one is likely to affect the other. Balance your attention between them and give yourself space to deal with disruptive events.

Some of our thinking can be likened to self-sabotage, so let's explore what this means, why it happens and what you can do to change it.

Self-sabotage

We all have our own assumptions about the way we approach our jobs. They might relate to the type of work we excel at or struggle with, the time of day when our concentration is either at its peak or shot to pieces, our management style, how we relate to other colleagues, or the value of our role in the organisation. Some can be fairly basic, such as a belief that we have to get through our To Do list each day, even if it means giving up our right to relax on an evening.

Assumptions can be positive and self-motivating: 'This project is my chance to shine', 'I'm good at explaining complex financial information to non-specialists', or 'I'm always able to come up with a creative solution to a problem'.

However, assumptions can also be negative: 'I'm not valued because I'm not on the leadership team'; 'I'll never master this system'; 'I can't write a report for toffee'; or 'the head will think I'm a slacker if I don't stay back after everyone else has gone home'. A lot of our self-sabotage is rooted in sky-high expectations of ourselves, way beyond what's really required. No wonder we feel inadequate.

Now for the hard question: are your assumptions misplaced? Always ask yourself this: are they helpful, or do they limit you?

Consider your To Do list: does it contain an unrealistic set of tasks, in volume or complexity? If so, no wonder you're struggling; you're setting yourself up to fail, especially if you don't know how long each task will take.

My biggest misplaced beliefs used to be that I had to do everything myself, complete my daily To Do list (which was full of unnecessary items and unrealistic self-imposed deadlines), and that everything had to be perfect. I've stayed up late at night, tinkering with a report, when the improvements didn't justify the extra effort. Then I struggled to maintain my concentration the next day. My approach was counterproductive.

It's not just the stories we tell ourselves which can cause problems; so can our outward behaviour. Can you think of an instance when you've over-reacted to someone who's spoken to you in a particular way, or when a sensitive subject has been discussed?

Early in my career, some people knew which buttons to press to make me argumentative or grumpy, usually by criticising me for something. I learned to spot when they were doing it and challenge them back in a thoughtful and rational way.

It's important to control your thoughts, otherwise you believe other people have the power to make you feel bad. You think your children are intent on stressing you out, when they're just 'being children' and not even giving you a thought. Perhaps you assume other people are winding you up, when it isn't their intention. You may be over-reacting because you're exhausted or on edge about something.

The good news is that you can change this. It's often more about the narrative you tell yourself, rather than any real character deficiencies. If you are aware of your tendencies you can watch out for the triggers, which is half the battle to stopping them. It will help you control your feelings next time and achieve a better outcome.

Challenge your assumptions

Let's look at an example of self-sabotage and consider how to resolve it, tough-love style. Let's examine the obsession with completing a To Do list no matter what it takes, even if it includes items devoid of importance or urgency. Why do you feel this way? What causes you to be so determined about it that you stay up late at night, pushing yourself so far that you can't function properly? If challenging yourself like this doesn't work, calculate your true hourly rate using your actual hours worked, and learn to value yourself more.

Try to stand back from it all and reflect on your assumptions. What's the worst that can happen if you don't complete every single item on the list? Are they all essential? Have you set realistic deadlines for them? Do you know how long each one will take?

Now consider the options. You can either accept not everything will get done (admittedly hard to do), or you can take action. Your aim should be to add only those tasks which a) are essential, and b) can only be done by you, then build a plan to achieve them in the time available. We'll work through this in a later chapter.

Learning to identify what isn't worthy of your attention is an important skill for your sanity. Imagine how much better you'll feel about your list if it's actually achievable. Successful people don't do everything themselves; they find other people to share the load.

Later on, we'll explore this properly, but suffice to say I've given up trying to do everything on my generic To Do list. Now it's just an aide-mémoire, a place to log items and ideas as they occur. I have a separate, extremely focused list of the most important things, and they always get done in the week or month they're scheduled for (except if there's an emergency). If something gets shunted down the list enough times, it wasn't important in the first place. I'll explain my methods later.

Now for our next two activities. You'll find them in the workbook with space to write your answers. This will encourage you to challenge yourself and identify potential changes to ease your stress.

Activity 3 - Negative beliefs

3.1 Make a list of any negative beliefs you hold. They can be from any part of your life. Are they self-sabotaging?
3.2 Write about why you believe each one. How does it make you feel? Does it limit you in any way?

Reflection

Did you come up with many negative beliefs? Did any of them surprise you?

For each one, write a note about an occasion when you were given evidence which contradicts it: an event, situation or conversation which showed you performed well or were appreciated.

For each contradictory example, how did it make you feel? Can you recognise and accept the positive evidence? For some reason we're often reluctant to give ourselves credit. Well, I'm giving you permission to do exactly that, in case you need it.

You should now be able to cross off some of the unhelpful beliefs, or at least know you can address them. This is a simple but effective way of changing your perceptions of yourself, which is a key ingredient of your mindset.

Activity 4 - Positive beliefs

4.1 Write a list of positive beliefs you hold about yourself.
4.2 For each one, write about why you believe it. How does it make you feel? Can you think of a time when it gave you the confidence to try something new, or approach something in a different way?

Affirmations like this are powerful, so if you have identified a positive belief which is linked to an important goal, write it on a piece of card and keep it somewhere handy to look at when you're in need of a boost. If you're feeling brave, put it on your wall, as long as it's not something like 'I'm better at finance than my headteacher' (unless they have a great sense of humour)!

Reflection
Consider your lists from activities 3 and 4. What's the overall balance between the two? Are there more positive or negative beliefs? Can you come up with any other ways to tackle the remaining negative beliefs and reinforce the positive ones?

If you are having a hard time over something, look back at your notes from this activity. Focus on the positive beliefs first, then your contradictory evidence on the negative beliefs. You can add more or repeat the exercise if it helps.

When things go wrong

A positive mindset is a huge help in challenging times. No one is perfect; we all get frazzled now and again, and everyone makes mistakes. When something goes wrong, you might experience a physical response. A knot builds up in the pit of my stomach and my face heats up. The sensation soon fades, but the embarrassment and guilt stay in my brain for ages afterwards.

It's OK to feel upset about something. Acknowledging it is part of the recovery process, and you need some 'me time' to come to terms with it. Writing about it by hand in a private notebook may make you feel better. Talking it over can also be helpful, but try not to go on about it for too long; constantly re-living it (wearing the 'victim t-shirt') will only make you feel worse. Once you've recognised it for what it is, a hopefully temporary setback, it's time to take action.

The first thing to consider is how serious the problem really is. Paul McGee recommends assigning a value to it between one and ten, where ten = death, then considering how you will feel about it in six months from now. This tip is in the '7 cartoons' download on his site.

Something that seems awful in the moment is usually soon forgotten by others. Yet you can hold it in your mind until it assumes an importance disproportionate to the actual event, and you carry on beating yourself up about it long afterwards. You really shouldn't torture yourself like this.

Secondly, decide how you're going to deal with it. Can you put it right, and if so, how and when? This is often the first reaction to an error, but if you act before processing your feelings and deciding how serious it is, you might attach a higher priority to it than it warrants. You might even keep the issue alive, which is not ideal!

If you are still struggling to get over a mistake, train yourself to regard it as a learning opportunity. Consider why it happened. Did you misunderstand what was expected of you? Did you have all the infor-mation you needed? Were you distracted by something else? Were you unable to devote sufficient time to it, or did you forget to prioritise it? Did you rely on information from someone else, who failed to provide it either accurately or in a timely manner?

The questions will vary depending on the situation, but knowing why and how it happened will help you get over it and be better prepared to deal with a similar situation in the future.

If it is down to you, be honest, but don't be too hard on yourself. Mistakes can easily happen, especially if you're trying to develop your skills or you're managing areas from another discipline. Apologising for a genuine error and finding ways to make sure it doesn't happen again are the best ways of getting through it.

In most situations there's a mix of reasons as to why problems occur, often linked to communication. If all else fails, recall all the mistakes others have made and you'll soon feel better!

Know when to stop

Do you understand what a task involves, step by step? One critical part of this is knowing the boundaries: when is a task complete?

Hands up all the perfectionists. Mine is in the air. How often do you continue to tinker with something, putting in extra effort for a gain so small that it won't be noticed? Do you realise how unproductive it is? By the time you finish something, circumstances might have changed, and it won't be fit for purpose. This is a mindset issue.

There's a phrase used by some productivity gurus that makes me twitchy: 'Done is better than perfect'. My perfectionist persona would argue it's simply not true; nothing can be better than perfection. But I concede it's more sensible. The art is judging when it's good enough.

I find the best way is to decide the purpose of your task and the level of detail it warrants. What will meet the needs of your intended audience? They'll be hoping for the simple version. Are you comfortable being identified as the person who's produced it, given the time you had available? If the answer is yes, then stop.

Timeliness is important. But what if a deadline is imposed by someone else? The same rule applies: know what the end product should look like, what you need to do to get to that stage, and how much time and effort it will take. Then stop at that point.

You could consult the person who gave you the task, to confirm the level of detail they want. This can save you a lot of effort. Long ago we did accruals for every item or service delivered but not paid for before 31st March. It was quite a revelation when auditors applied a significance threshold to accruals, and the closure workload plummeted! It made perfect sense, when balances were carried forward.

This was an external decision, but my point is that attitudes can change, so don't assume the requirements will stay the same. If you check your understanding and offer an alternative suggestion, they might realise they've been clinging on to the old ways and be ready to accept a better, more efficient method.

Productivity in a crisis

In a book written in 2020, I can't ignore the Coronavirus crisis. This has turned our world upside down, and schools have been in the front line, helping key worker parents to continue doing their jobs. It has brought huge uncertainty and complexity to daily routines. My Thursday evening applause was for school staff as well as the NHS.

However your routine changed, you will have handled the situation in your own way. Perhaps you obsessed about being up to date, or couldn't cope with too much information and hid from it all.

This sort of situation forces us to rethink our approach to productivity. My advice would be don't worry about whatever anyone else is doing. You do things your way, and be kind to yourself.

Coping strategies

In April 2020, I led a webinar for Schools North East, 'Coping in a Crisis', focused on the Coronavirus situation. The main strategies I covered can be applied to any crisis. I'll also refer to some of these in later chapters, but reinforcement is a good learning strategy!

- *Self-care*

The most important response to a crisis is to practise self-care. Forget the superhero act. Whether it's a short-term emergency or a longer-term crisis, you're bound to have an emotional response to it. We all cope in different ways. Keep an eye open for those who start behaving differently; they may need some support.

Make sure your diet is nutritious, and get enough rest, sleep, hydration, and exercise. But also make space for leisure pursuits. Rest your mind, use deep breathing to stay calm, practise meditation, write in a journal to get thoughts and fears out of your brain, or talk to others. Your subconscious needs time to mull over your problems, and it can't do that if your brain is constantly running at 110 mph.

- *Focus on what matters*

Pay attention to the things you can control and try to accept or ignore those you can't. Identify the top priorities for now, and acknowledge that you'll need to let some routine things slip. People will understand, and you will catch up at some point. Assess the effort a task will take compared to its impact, and don't worry about unnecessary details. Keep minor tasks out of your important and urgent list, and delegate jobs to others wherever possible. Re-assess risks according to the emergency.

- *Adjust your working practices*

Working from home can bring benefits and challenges; I've addressed this in a separate section.

Accountability has a high profile in education, but an emergency changes the rules. Review whether goals are realistic, ensure everyone has access to the information they need to complete their tasks, and review success measures and deadlines for relevance.

Communication is vital in a crisis. Make sure everyone is coping, and be clear about when rules are being relaxed or enforced. Some schools hold weekly well-being calls on online platforms, which are invaluable as a space where work isn't discussed.

- *Get support*

When you're on a plane and the cabin crew are doing their emergency demo, what do they say? Fit your own oxygen mask first before helping others. We'd all do well to remember this, not only in times of crisis but in ordinary times too.

Ask for help, at work and at home. Use virtual networks; there's a fabulous SBP community on Twitter, providing moral and emotional support as well as practical problem solving. There's always someone who's experienced what you're going through. Make sure you know what financial and in-kind support you can get, and find stress relief techniques which work for you.

- *Anticipate the 'new normal'*

This depends on the length of the emergency. During the Coronavirus lockdown, journalists speculated about when schools would accept more pupils well before it was due to happen, which wound everyone up. I'm not suggesting you worry about the end of a crisis while you're in it, but some low-key preparation will make you feel more ready for it. Thinking about the 'new normal' possibilities will help your subconscious work on it and find creative solutions.

You will be able to identify things you'll do differently in future; a crisis often exposes weaknesses in systems and processes which can be rectified.

Of course you will have a business continuity plan (BCP), but I imagine a pandemic like Coronavirus wasn't anticipated when it was written. Is your BCP is fit for purpose and do colleagues know how to play their part in following it? Once an emergency is over, make any necessary changes.

Working from home

You don't need a crisis situation to justify working from home; it can be a useful way of getting important projects and tasks done in normal times. At least it won't involve home schooling your children!

Home has been my office base for five years now. It took me a while to adjust, so don't expect to feel comfortable immediately. It's your place to relax, so working there can change the dynamic.

You might struggle to find an ideal spot to work in. For ages, I used my dining room table, despite the disruption of having to move my IT kit whenever I needed to serve a meal. After my husband retired, I set up an office in a spare bedroom. Cue a trip to a certain Swedish store for a desk and chair. It's made a big difference to my mindset; once I sit down, I start working straight away.

There are some things you can do to ease the transition. Establishing a routine is vital. It will stop you sliding into bad habits and create a disciplined atmosphere so you can focus on the task that was the reason for escaping the office. If you don't get it done at home, you have no excuse!

Set out a schedule for yourself, with regular breaks to drink water, stretch and move away from your computer screen. Take a proper lunch break and fit in a walk. By the way, it shouldn't be impossible to do all this on the days when you're in school either!

A daily walk on the beach has such a positive impact on my energy and motivation. I listen to podcasts while I walk, so I'm learning too. It releases tension and refreshes me, sending me back to the laptop with enthusiasm for the afternoon session.

Remember there will be struggles; it's part and parcel of life. Not everything goes according to plan, and sometimes you have no control over what happens. Be courageous, and show determination and persistence. You'll win in the end. This is why goals are so important; they give you a focal point which helps you to keep going in the face of challenges.

Key points

- Being aware of your mindset is the first step towards changing your thinking, which helps you address the internal barriers to productivity.
- Learn to control your response to a situation and keep a balanced perspective on it.

- Tackle self-sabotage by challenging your negative beliefs and misplaced assumptions, and find the positives instead.
- When things go wrong, acknowledge them and take a proportionate view: how bad is it, honestly? How can you put it right and move on? Can you see it as a learning opportunity?
- Know when to stop: scope out your tasks, set boundaries and don't keep tinkering for a minimal gain.
- Ramp up the self-care in a crisis to help you cope. Focus on what matters, adjust your working practices, and get support. Do some gentle thinking about what the 'new normal' might be.

4

SELF-CARE

Health and performance

If you are not at your best, you won't perform well. It may be obvious, yet we still push ourselves without realising how unproductive it is.

So here's the 'tough love' reality. If you're exhausted, you'll find it harder to concentrate. Silly mistakes could harm your reputation for being accurate and reliable and others might lose faith in you.

You'll also find it harder to get the most out of your team or colleagues; if we're tired, we tend to find faults in others more readily. This can set off a cycle of defensiveness and mistrust, which isn't good if you need support for an important project or task.

Both physical and mental health are essential for navigating all the challenges in our life. Think back to a time when you've been ill. Was it at the start of a holiday period? Had you been working flat out to complete a project or trying to manage multiple deadlines? This happens regularly to my friends who are teachers or school business managers. It's as if their body says 'Right, I've had enough of being pushed at this pace, and now we're on a break, I'm going to force you to take it easy.' If you listen to your body, it will tell you when you need to slow down. Ignore the signals at your peril.

By riding on a wave of adrenaline, we can complete a lot in a relatively short time. Positive pressure comes from within, from wanting to do our best, and we tap into it to achieve our goals. It isn't a problem in the short term; it's only when it tips over the edge and becomes a longer-term habit that it turns into stress. When an adrenaline rush goes on too long then stops, we become more vulnerable to infections and tiredness. We've exhausted all our natural reserves of energy and have over-stretched our immune system.

Developing practices to create a strong foundation in your body and mind will help you cope, allowing you to tackle the causes of your stress before you go under.

Think about how you can be more intentional about improving your approach. Make appointments with yourself in your diary as you would for meetings with other people. Making time for yourself isn't a crime. Self-care is vital, a long-term protection against illness (physical and mental), and you owe it to yourself to make it a priority.

Physical health

First, a disclaimer: I am not a doctor and you shouldn't treat this as medical advice. There are many sources of information on physical health by qualified professionals, so I can only cover general topics.

Self-awareness is vital; pay attention to your mind and body and know when to seek medical help. You are not wasting the doctor's time; if you ignore symptoms and things get worse, you are likely to suffer more, and you might face a prolonged period of illness.

If you are still resisting, think on: if it leads to you taking sick leave, it could have a potentially significant impact on your organisation. Furthermore, should you need hospital treatment, you will put additional pressure on the NHS. Sorry to be blunt, but some people just won't look after themselves!

Diet is obviously vital to your well-being. There are conflicting messages about what's good or bad, so finding what suits you can be a case of trial and error. Pay attention to your body and notice any changes. You may have a condition which is exacerbated when you eat a particular food. Work out how you feel after a meal; it may give you some clues about where your diet isn't doing you any favours.

Don't hesitate to go to your doctor if you can't identify why you're not feeling your normal self. If you have a health condition, take your medication regularly and return to your doctor if it's not working.

Do you make sure you drink enough water during the day to help you stay alert? Keeping a water bottle on your desk acts as a reminder, or you can use a fitness tracker app.

Stress can have a detrimental effect on our physical health as well as our mental state; it lowers immunity, making you more susceptible to infections and other physical illnesses. Last year, two writers I know each had a mini-stroke. Both were in their mid-forties and had ignored all the warning signs. The story of one of them was in the press (link).

We take our car for its MOT every year once it's over three years old. So why wouldn't we take the same approach for our own bodily health? Do you have regular check ups, including eye, hearing and dental tests, and well man/woman screening?

If you have long-term health conditions, make sure your employer knows, so they can make necessary adjustments such as time off for medical appointments or occasional working from home.

Posture

The human body isn't suited to sitting for long periods; office workers can be prone to back and neck problems. Make sure your back is straight and imagine a thread pulling your head up. Your chair needs to provide good lumbar support.

I believe laptops are misnamed, because they should not be used on your lap. Doing so caused me back spasms and permanent pain; I didn't know that constantly looking down puts too much strain on your neck and spine. A strong prescription gave me enough relief to walk and stretch, then I learned to manage my condition naturally.

Now I have an adjustable Nexstand laptop stand (link) with a separate wireless mouse and keyboard (link), which allow me to keep the screen at eye level when sitting or standing.

Yoga and Pilates can help, with a qualified and experienced instructor. I've found yoga relaxing and energising, and walking also helps. However, exercise may not be a solution for everyone with back pain; it's vital to get a proper diagnosis and expert help to determine the best treatment for you.

Repetitive strain injury (RSI) is another risk when using a computer for long periods. If you start to suffer, see your GP before it becomes too painful. An ergonomic mouse, a mouse pad with a gel cushion or a wrist support for your keyboard can help lessen the symptoms, but you might need treatment.

With any problems like these, a preventative approach is best. Ask for a workplace assessment to check if your set up is right for you; your employer has a duty to make any necessary adjustments.

Dictation

Dictation can help prevent back problems and RSI; you can stand or walk around with a Bluetooth headset or lavalier microphone. Even if you do a lot of figurework, you can dictate reports and emails.

Many dictation (Speech to Text) applications are free, but have varying success rates. I use Dragon dictation software by Nuance (link), which is very accurate once you've taken time to train it. It is compatible with most programmes including the full Office suite, Google Docs, email and websites. The desktop version is Windows only, but the Dragon Anywhere version works on other devices.

You need a quiet place, or you can go walking and use a digital voice recorder with a USB connector. Plug it into your computer when you return, and Dragon transcribes it in an instant. But a thorough edit is always needed; there can be some funny typos!

If you are a speedy typist, it might not be faster, but it's worth being proactive to prevent physical problems like back pain or RSI.

Sleep

Sleep has so many benefits that it's become an obsession. Your body and your mind both regenerate during sleep, like rebooting your internal computer. It also strengthens your immune system. Conversely, a lack of sleep can impair your judgement.

My sleep problems were worse during challenging periods at work. My mind used to buzz around like an annoying fly, going over and over all my worries. The more frustrated I got about not being able to drop off, the harder it was to give in, even when exhausted.

I hope the tips and techniques in this book will help you overcome your own workload problems if they're stopping you from getting a good night's sleep. But there are some short-term solutions. Many experts recommend sleep hygiene, which is just another way of describing your routines before bedtime. Are you increasing your chances of sleeping by preparing for it?

Try some of the following practices:

- no computer/mobile/tablet screens an hour before bed;
- during the evening, plan a broad outline for tomorrow;
- set out your clothes and bag for the next day;
- drink a little water;
- do a few stretches and some slow, controlled breathing;
- go to bed at a regular time;
- make sure the room is dark;
- focus on your breathing to help you fall asleep.

An excessively active mind is a common barrier to sleep. Here are some tactics which have helped me.

- A lavender pillow spray, Deep Sleep Pillow Spray by 'thisworks' (link).
- Writing about any worries before I go to sleep: what happened, how I feel about it, why I won't let it bother me and how I can resolve it. Then I symbolically close the notebook on it.
- If I wake up in the middle of the night, remembering

something I should have done, I write it down rather than lie there thinking about it.

- Instead of tossing and turning in bed, I get up and go into another room to read a chapter of a book, then return to bed. Making a fresh attempt is better than lying there, getting more and more frustrated about not sleeping.

One of the causes of poor sleep can be discomfort. When did you last change your mattress? Do you have the right number of pillows and are they the right thickness? Is the room too hot or too cold? Be more like Goldilocks!

Exercise

Whatever your fitness level, you should be able to do some movement. If you have health conditions or a disability, please get advice from your GP on what you are able to do and what you should avoid.

You may need to be creative to fit in some exercise. On a morning, can you park at a distance from school and walk the rest of the way, or arrive earlier and go for a walk around the block? You'll not only benefit physically from the exercise, but you'll also be more alert.

Why not take a lunchtime walk? I bet there's nothing in your contract to stop you leaving the site, unless you do dinner duty. Build some movement into your daily tasks. Batch your visits around the site to spend a good chunk of time walking around. You could go for a walk at the end of the day before you climb into your car and drive home. It may help you put your worries into perspective.

Do you have a meeting arranged with someone? Could you agree to convert it into a walking meeting? Record action points in a voice app on your phone and note them in your planner on your return.

You may believe you can't possibly make space for exercise, but have you really tried? There are so many options, some with social interaction which adds a feel-good factor. If you have children, think creatively about how you can best use the time you spend with them to get fitter yourself. Mine were easier to amuse outside or on a walk.

If you try some of my suggestions on working more efficiently, you should be able to organise the rest of your day so that you can avoid using your leisure time to catch up on unfinished business. Others manage it, so why shouldn't you?

Mental and emotional health

Mental and emotional health is just as fundamental to our performance at work as physical health, and more so for many people. I'm referring to our general moods and resilience. The stresses and strains of daily life can get even the most resilient people down from time to time, and just one tiny additional irritant can tip the balance.

Another disclaimer: I'm not a health professional. You must get professional help for mental health conditions. Don't be embarrassed about asking for support; there are plenty of treatments available.

Unless you regularly make time to relax, you may not fully appreciate the benefits. It's far too easy to push yourself, barely noting the sense of achievement as you tick an item off the To Do list before moving on to the next one, conscious of another deadline looming.

I've been in enough school offices to see the host of interruptions an SBP is plagued with throughout the day; we'll look at some solutions to this later. More often than not, you go home without having completed what you'd planned. You continue working into the evening and eventually fall into bed exhausted. You toss and turn, your brain still processing the day's events. The next morning, you're tired before you've even done anything. It's a vicious circle.

The lessons I've learned

Over-working is counterproductive. I've done it, working evenings and weekends and squeezing in family life around my job. In 2008, I was diagnosed with possible endometrial cancer. My consultant rushed me into a hysterectomy (at the word cancer, I turned into a compliant mess), and I was off sick for three months. The suspicious cells were found to be pre cancerous, but it was still a wake-up call, a reminder of my mortality.

During the early part of my enforced absence, physical movement was strictly limited to gentle walks. I enjoyed some previous hobbies, then returned to work and vowed I would never let my job take over again. But it wasn't that easy.

At last I listened to myself, and applied for early retirement. I became a freelance consultant, freeing up time to spend with my daughter and new granddaughter. Then, together with Nikola Flint, I started School Financial Success, with a desire to help others navigate their way through the maze of education funding.

My situation and choices will be different to yours, but the main point I'm making is that you need to listen to your body and brain, and act as soon as you feel out of kilter.

Mentally healthy habits

Be intentional about cultivating healthy habits. Try different things, find out what works, and make the changes gradually. Don't let your leisure activities be the first things you give up when you're under pressure. Preserve them as the foundation of your well-being.

Resting is under-rated. Being busy is somehow seen as a virtue, even if it's unproductive. Slowing down can be difficult, but we're not talking about total inaction, just switching off your worries for a short period each day. Don't be consumed with guilt about it, just do it.

What does your morning routine look like? Do you pick up your phone as soon as you wake up? Do you read all the negative news stories, or absorb everyone else's noise on social media?

Make a small investment in yourself each day before you do anything else. It could be as simple as a quiet cuppa and some thinking space before anyone else wakes up, reading a couple of pages of a book, or doing a short meditation. Do whatever gets you in a positive, happy place to start your day.

Do you tie yourself in knots worrying about something someone has said to you? You could write a letter to the person who's upset you, setting out all your feelings. Can you understand their perspective and forgive them? It can help you move on. When you've finished, do not send it; symbolically tear your letter into little pieces and throw it away, telling yourself that's the end of it.

Sometimes self-care is about doing something difficult. You know it's good for you, but you might not feel like doing it. Addressing procrastination is a good example; we get comfortable in our habits and it can be hard to change. Never fear, I have some ideas later!

Supportive friends and family

Friends and family should be your allies when you're trying to balance your life; it should improve things for you all. Sometimes they may seem unsupportive, but if you explain what you're trying to do and why, you will hopefully get them on your side. Pick a moment when everyone is calm, and you're more likely to succeed.

The nature of family life and friendship is that sad and troubling things will happen along with the joy. There will be conflict, illnesses, disasters and bereavements. Managing these while holding down a responsible job isn't easy, is it? At the time you can be in despair, but most events are temporary and will be resolved or accepted eventually. It's a matter of trying to do the right thing.

Let your manager know if you're going through a tough period. You may be able to take special leave or unpaid leave; some things are more important than money. I'm sure you'd react in a supportive way if it was one of your staff, so don't treat yourself any differently. Self-care means giving others the chance to help you when you need it.

If you have children (of any age), it's incredibly difficult to do anything for yourself. I know; my twin sons were born when my daughter was just two, and I can't remember much about my daily routines with three under-threes!

Whatever choices you make about your balance between work and family, whether it's your working patterns or childcare arrangements, never let yourself feel guilty or inadequate, and don't apologise for your decisions. Do what's right for you and your family.

. . .

Find your community

Humans have always gathered in groups, and now it seems even more important. Your family and friends might not share all your interests, but you can look elsewhere.

Have you found your community? Having others who understand what you're dealing with is vital when you're going through a difficult time. You might have local networks (if not, start one!), or you could look to social media platforms. Twitter has a vibrant SBL/SBM community, which Hilary Goldsmith has now extended to the SBL Connect website and forum (link). You may know of other groups.

The DfE has put together a list of regional SBP networks (link) and you can sign up for a newsletter with occasional information about initiatives to help SBPs. Local groups provide the chance to meet in person and make strong connections.

Although conferences require time and money, and you can usually find online alternatives, a day out of the office can provide a breather and a chance to put things in perspective by talking face to face with your peers, as well as learning something new.

Activity 5 - Handling pressure

5.1 Make a list of the situations which cause you to feel under pressure, at work or at home. Do they have anything in common? Can you work out any ways of preventing them?
5.2 Now think about how you handle the situations on your list. Could you do things differently next time? How? What sources of support might be available to you?
5.3 What healthy habits can you develop, to increase your resilience and enable you to bounce back from difficult times?

Relaxation

Learning to relax takes perseverance, but it's definitely worthwhile. Being stressed and over-stimulated is exhausting. I've found the most helpful techniques for slowing down have been meditation and free writing. So I thought it was worth sharing a little about them.

Meditation

I'm a logical person and sceptical about things I can't prove with data and reasoning. But meditation has helped me to be more aware of my inner state, the calmness bringing inspiration and solutions.

It's simple to practise: find a quiet spot, settle yourself into a comfortable position and slow down your breathing. Become mindful of your surroundings, noticing the sights and sounds around you. Close your eyes and summon up a word or phrase, repeating it silently in your head. Focus on the silence and emptiness. If thoughts come, acknowledge they are there, then dismiss them and regain your focus.

Meditation may take a while to get used to if you're new to it or returning after a gap. I felt awkward and unsure at first. Each session may bring a different experience, but showing up regularly helps.

If you're stressed, you can also use deep breathing without meditation to help you relax.

Free writing

Through writing we can get a deeper understanding of ourselves, which is why a technique called free writing can help our emotional health. Journalling is similar. Our conscious mind self-censors and criticises, so for a deeper understanding, we need to access our subconscious mind. Free writing is like taking dictation from your brain.

Writing down all your negative ideas and emotions gets them out of your mind and can lessen their hold on you. It helps you separate your reactions from the events which have caused them (remember

The Sumo Guy's suggestions). I was sceptical at first, but it definitely works; ideas come to the surface that I'd never have had otherwise.

By free writing regularly, you can see themes emerging, analyse them and build or strengthen trust in your own instincts. What better excuse to buy a nice notebook, my fellow stationery addicts?

Simply find paper and a pen or pencil, and set aside fifteen minutes, or decide on a number of pages to fill. Relax with deep breaths, then write as fast as you can. Keep your hand moving. You can write about a question, a dilemma or a recent interaction with someone, or just start writing and see what comes out.

Don't think, just write. Don't stop to read what you've written or judge what emerges, and don't cross anything out. Spelling, punctuation and grammar don't matter (the only time I'll ever say this!). If you get stuck, describe your surroundings or write nonsense, until a thought comes to you.

Try to capture the details of what you see, hear, feel or think. Be brave and truthful; your subconscious is working through something. No one will see it (hide your notebook if needed). Keep going, even if it's boring. Something will emerge once you get past the surface.

This is a much better way of processing your angst, disappointment or anger about something than bottling it all up or taking it out on someone. Why not give it a go and see if it helps?

Making time to relax

I hope you can accept the need for relaxation time. It doesn't have to take long, but there will be a cumulative benefit.

Book it in your diary and organise everything else around it. Then keep the appointments with yourself. You wouldn't let down your employer or a friend if you arranged a meeting unless there was an emergency, would you? Well then, don't let yourself down.

It's amazing what you can fit in if you are determined about it. I don't enjoy cooking, so I listen to podcasts at the same time. The rhythmic movement of knitting helps my subconscious to produce ideas and solutions. Phone apps like Kindle, Apple Books and Kobo (ebooks), or Audible and Findaway Voices (audiobooks), allow me to read or listen to books while travelling.

Remember what you used to enjoy doing before life got hectic, and connect with local groups (whatever is possible post-Coronavirus). Having a group of friends who enjoy doing the same things will make you want to turn up, instead of making excuses to stay at home and do more work.

Key points

- Physical, mental and emotional health are the foundations of productivity and performance; listen to your body and mind and address any problems. Act quickly if you need medical help.
- Discover the most effective nutritious diet for you, stay hydrated, and have regular check ups.
- Keep an eye on your posture, to avoid neck and back pain, repetitive strain injury or other related conditions.
- Harness the benefits of sleep by practising sleep hygiene and writing down your worries before bedtime. Rest when you can, to 'reboot' your internal computer.
- Be creative about making room in your schedule for exercise.
- Pay particular attention to mental and emotional health to reduce stress. Find sources of support (your community, family and friends), create mentally healthy habits and learn to relax.

5

KNOW YOURSELF

Your inner voice

Self-awareness is a great tool for improving your productivity, because it guides you to make the right decisions and avoid mistakes.

Be honest with yourself. Do you need to let something go that isn't working? Are you stuck in a loop, unable to achieve your ambitions? Is there something new you've always wanted to try? Your inner voice will pipe up, sometimes without you knowing where the thoughts have come from. Pay attention to it.

I speak from experience. My church set up a Restoration Fund to repair the stonework, and in a meeting I somehow found myself saying: 'We could write a parish history and sell it.' I'd never written a book before. They said 'Go on then,' and it set me off on my author journey. I wouldn't be writing this now if that hadn't happened!

You will probably know instinctively when you haven't done your best work. We're all human, and mistakes happen, so don't be too harsh on yourself. Watch out for the feeling and use it as an alert mechanism to spot when things start to go wrong. Sense checking is an important final step when you've been doing a piece of analysis.

. . .

Taking decisions

Instinct plays an important part in decision-making. Trust your inner voice, test it against all the information you have, and make a decision you know you can live with. Remember, you can only deal with what you know at the time; use your experience as a guide.

Sometimes you may feel a strong sense of discomfort about what someone else is asking you to do. You might not have a choice; you're told to do it. Have you said anything? To be truly productive, you need to be free of distractions. Having something on your conscience, regretting either action or inaction, can play havoc with your focus.

If you're in this situation, you can always draw the other person's attention to the Nolan '7 Principles of Public Life' (link), if what they're proposing goes against the acceptable standards and you want to make them re-think.

When I haven't challenged someone over an action I disagree with, I can brood over it for ages. It's hard to concentrate on other essential pieces of work. I have to resolve it with the person involved before I can move on, but it would have been far better to make the challenge straight away. You may react differently.

There are unfortunate examples of staff in schools mismanaging resources and ignoring rules. Financial Notices to Improve (link) or financial management and governance review reports published by the Education & Skills Funding Agency (link) provide salutary lessons and help you be proactive in avoiding trouble.

If you see bad decisions, consider what the consequences might be. If it's a low-key, one-off incident, you may be able to ask a trusted person for help to stop it. Alternatively, you could have a quiet word with the person involved. It all depends on the circumstances.

If it's more serious, such as a suspected fraud, racism or bullying of staff, you need to report it and make sure action is taken. There are protections against whistle blowers, but it can still feel risky, so find someone to support you: a union or reliable colleague.

Although it can be daunting to tackle problems like these, by not taking action and letting the behaviour continue, you may see others suffer. In most instances it's likely to be low-level concerns, but in a minority of cases things can become serious. There are plenty of media reports which show the impact of this on all concerned.

This is relevant to productivity because it's better to prevent such issues than having to take action after the event. I've carried out enough disciplinary investigations to know how time-consuming and stressful they can be for all those involved. Many years ago, one ended in me giving evidence to the General Teaching Council.

What energises you?

To perform well, we need to sustain our energy levels, not only in a physical sense, but to keep a clear sense of purpose, an inner motivation and enthusiasm for our work. We all need to 're-fill the well' regularly, to prepare for future challenges.

When we're energised, ideas seem to flow more naturally. Our creativity and problem solving ability are stronger and our confidence soars. It's a wonderful feeling, but it's hard to sustain for a long time if you haven't got a core source of energy.

Make the most of the times when you are in this happy state. Write down ideas as they come to you and put them in a safe place. Refer to them when you are doing your planning, especially if you're stuck over something. Even an idea on the list which is unrelated to your current task might resonate and spark a new idea.

Listen to yourself and notice what energises you. What do you most enjoy doing? Is there something you used to love but haven't tried for ages? It all helps with balancing your life.

I've sung in our church choir for over twenty years, but last year I joined Hartlepool Ladies' Choir and I love it (or did before Coronavirus intervened). There's a sense of achievement in learning complex harmonies and performing at venues like The Sage at Gateshead, the Royal Albert Hall and local community groups.

What about the people in your professional and personal life? Who are they, and what is it about them and their interaction with you that gives you energy? Maybe they help you see the funny side of things, or they don't judge you, but give unconditional love and support. These and many other aspects are all important in helping you keep a positive frame of mind and staying resilient.

If you are introverted, it doesn't necessarily mean you are shy and retiring. It's more about whether being with other people energises you or drains you. For example, you may need space to recover from big events or meetings compared to extroverts.

I encourage you to pay attention to how you balance all aspects of your life as well as improving your work practices. It's when you are intentional about it, identifying what needs to change and taking steps to make it happen, that you'll achieve a better mix.

Activity 6 - What energises you?

6.1 Take a few minutes to make a list of the people and/or things which energise you.
6.2. Can you identify why they have this effect?
6.3. Can you put into words how they make you feel?

Reflection

Do some writing about how you could make more space for the people and pursuits you've listed, and whether there are any other activities which would have the same effect. Keep this list in mind when you are building your goals in the next chapter.

What drains you?

When you have a demanding job, it can take over your life and sap your energy. There will be times when it's hard to motivate yourself to do your best work. You are likely to be more disorganised than usual, which makes it hard to sustain your good reputation.

This is often about being pulled out of your comfort zone. It's good to be stretched, because it's where growth happens. But if it's too big a leap, it can be overwhelming and counterproductive.

When scheduling your work to meet deadlines, break down new and/or large tasks into smaller chunks which you can tackle when you're in a positive, energised frame of mind. First, make sure you have the knowledge, skills and information to complete a task, otherwise you will be daunted and easily defeated by it.

But don't take this too far. Learn just enough. Don't gather a lot of information you don't need yet; you'll find yourself afflicted by analysis paralysis, where you become confused by it all. If you ask enough people, you'll get lots of conflicting views.

Complex work can be tiring. If you sense your attention wandering, get up, stretch your legs, and have a glass of water or a piece of fruit. Depending on your deadlines, you can either return to it or do something different for a while before resuming the task.

The other side of the coin is work which is simple but repetitive and boring. Is there a particular task you hate doing, something soul-destroying? I've known a fair few in my career, from going down to a dark basement to look up invoices, to doing technical updates on my websites. Save less important tasks for periods when your energy drops, but don't put them off for too long.

Meetings which go on for ages and never seem to achieve anything can be draining. I confess that on a few occasions boredom led me to work out the cost of the meeting in attendees' salaries (a privileged hobby for those who compile a budget)! You can't stop those who like the sound of their own voice, but you can control your own input. If you can't add anything significant, stay quiet. Avoid getting drawn into discussions on side issues. You'll find people will respect you and pay more attention to you because you're concise and direct. When you do speak, it will be worth their while to listen.

We all know people who drain us if we're around them for too long. It can be hard to be polite when they collar you, usually at the precise moment when there's something important waiting for your attention. Sometimes you can't avoid them or escape from them, but where you have a choice, think carefully about accepting invitations to be with them. No one has a right to monopolise your time, especially if they are unpleasant or relentlessly negative. It will rub off on you.

Activity 7 - What drains you?

7.1 Make a list of people, tasks and anything else which drains you.
7.2 How do they make you feel?
7.3 Why do they have this effect?
7.4 What could you do about it?

Key points

- Self-awareness helps you make good (and productive) decisions, so listen to your inner voice when you're feeling uncomfortable about something and act on it.
- Knowing yourself means you can trust your instincts, and you will sense when things are starting to go wrong. But don't be too harsh on yourself if you make mistakes.
- Reflect on what energises you and learn to make time for it. Log the ideas that come when you're energised. If you 're-fill the well' regularly, you'll replenish your reserves and be ready for future challenges.
- Understand why you are drained by some things or people, and avoid them wherever possible.

6

HABITS

To achieve our goals, we need to follow the steps that will produce the right results. But motivating ourselves to perform the actions can drain our energy and it's hard to sustain performance for a long time. So to become more productive, we need to find ways of making it easier. The solution is to develop the right habits.

Habits come in all shapes and sizes and appear in every part of your life. They can be good or bad; the key is to recognise them and decide which ones you should change to make the biggest difference.

The word habit sounds a little constricting, doesn't it? But changing your habits will bring you freedom, by giving you more choice over your life. Removing those which cause negativity or discomfort and replacing them with positive behaviours will create a better mindset, more energy, and improved time management.

Habits are not only personal; they can apply to teams or whole organisations. Think about this topic not only in terms of the way you operate, but also how your team(s) and school work. It's powerful to realise you can get a different result simply by changing the way everyone responds to situations. Why not identify some pinch points in your processes where things stick, or where there's conflict, and try some of the tips in this chapter? It could provide a helpful focus for performance management discussions.

Awareness of habits

The first step is to become aware of the habits you have, and decide whether they're constructive or destructive. What's the balance, and what can you stop doing, minimise or do more of? Consciously watching for habits and recording when you do them will give you an idea of what you need to pay attention to.

For example, if you find your concentration wandering and you pick up your phone to go on social media, does it always happen at the same point? Is it at a specific time of day, or when you're tackling a particular type of task? Is the task boring, or are you doing it in a long stretch without a break?

A reasonable pause for refreshment, a stretch and some movement is fine, but not if it ends up with you spending half an hour more on your phone looking at cat or dog videos. It's better to switch to a different but necessary task in the blocks of time when you should be working.

Later I'll share my system, which involves planners from Productive Flourishing (link). Their website says this:

'Habits are powerful because they create defaults... Some habits are incredibly empowering, but we don't realize their strength until they're absent. And, since many of our destructive habits are tied to deep physical, emotional, or social desires, we quickly return to them.'

Habits may seem small in themselves, but they build up and multiply like compound interest on savings (a lot faster, in fact, given current interest rates!). It doesn't matter how big the habit is, it's the repetition which makes it work. When you first change a habit, you may not see a lot of difference at first. But if you keep at it, the benefits will grow over time. It's like the days when cars stalled or broke down, and needed a push to get going. It's a terrible strain at first, but once the wheels start moving, it picks up momentum and gets easier.

Trying to lose weight is an obvious example. You cut out food items and reduce your portion sizes, but when you stand on the scales after the first week, your weight hasn't changed. After a while, you reach a tipping point, when the pounds start to drop off and you feel better.

Years ago, there was an experiment where children were offered the choice of eating one marshmallow now or waiting and having two. The researchers tracked the children afterwards, and those who'd been patient and waited for two marshmallows tended to do better in life than the others. Nowadays, everyone wants results straight away, but patience and consistency will get you a lot further in the long run. It takes time to build a habit; some experts say it takes 66 days on average.

To be successful in changing your habits, you need to be single-minded about wanting to change. The goal has to be something you really want, otherwise it's hard to find the motivation to make the changes.

The elements of habits

Many years ago, I read 'The Power of Habit' by Charles Duhigg (link) and found it fascinating. He says habits emerge without our conscious consent because they are the brain's way of protecting itself from all the demands we're placing on it. It's conserving energy to make the important decisions, by thinking about what worked before and then implementing it.

Duhigg describes three aspects to a habit: the cue, the routine and the reward.

I'm going to make a confession about a personal habit to explain this. On a morning, I do my important tasks, often large projects like a consultancy assignment or drafting a book. Mid-way through the session, I begin to lose interest and need a break. I make a cup of coffee, and I've got into the habit of eating a Stroopwafel (yes, just one, but have you seen the size of them?). Obviously it's my husband's fault for buying them. I need to tackle this habit to avoid putting on weight. Sorry if this isn't as exciting as you expected it to be!

The cue is a situation or event which triggers a habit, telling the brain to go into automatic mode. It can be a location, a specific time of day, a sensory stimulus, a thought, or an action (either conscious or automatic). When you feel an urge like reaching for a chocolate bar, what's just happened? Where are you? What time is it? Who is nearby? What did you just do? What emotion are you feeling? One or more of these five things is the cue that makes you do the habit.

My cue is a mid-morning weariness from working on one task.

The routine is the behaviour or action you take in response to the cue. It involves creating a reward for yourself;: it can be physical, mental or emotional. It soon becomes hardwired into your brain, like brushing your teeth after breakfast every day.

My routine is making the cup of coffee and reaching for the packet of Stroopwafels while the kettle is boiling.

The reward is the pleasure you feel as a result of your action. It's a way of satisfying the craving which led you to the habit, telling the brain the habit is worth repeating. The craving is what cements the habit into your day. Try to identify what the craving is, by substituting a different reward. If the new reward doesn't satisfy it, keep trying until you find a better one.

My reward is eating the Stroopwafel. They are seriously yummy!

You have several options for breaking a habit. If you are strong willed, the easiest is to change the routine when you recognise the cue. Instead of making the cup of coffee, I could take a bottle of water to my office to last me the morning, then I wouldn't be led to the kitchen and tempted to find the biscuits. Or I could bypass the kitchen and go for a quick walk around the garden.

Another approach would be to change the cue and/or the reward. To tackle my cue, I could perk myself up by switching to another task. This doesn't always work for me, because sometimes I need a longer period of concentration to finish a piece of financial analysis or complete a chapter. If I leave it, I know it will take me longer to get back into the flow when I return to it. I've changed the reward, keeping the coffee and gradually reducing the Stroopwafel to every 2 or 3 days. I'm steeling myself to replace them with fruit eventually!

Once you've chosen your cue and reward, you need to decide this:

'When (cue) happens, I will (do the new routine) because it provides me with (the reward).'

It may take a while to get into the new habit, but once you start repeating it, I assure you it will get easier. I appreciate my Stroopwafel more now than when it was a daily habit.

Make changes

Understanding why you need to change

Having a reason for changing a habit or beginning one motivates you to persist when it gets tough, as inevitably happens. Will a new habit make you feel better, such as taking a daily walk? Could it stop you procrastinating, so you finish your tasks sooner and get home on time, such as removing the Facebook app from your phone? Would a 'shut-down' routine help you relax on an evening and sleep more deeply, so you wake refreshed the following morning?

Once you recognise patterns in your behaviour as positive or negative, you can do something about them and be more in control.

Creating new constructive habits

For real change, try to build constructive habits which you do without thinking. If you remove the effort from the process, it will be easier to embed them in your daily life.

One such habit is to clear your 'mental inbox' at the start of the day, when you're in the shower or travelling to work. What do you have planned? Are you tackling the right things in the right order and in the most productive way? Remind yourself of the tips and tricks you'll use, like sorting emails and not responding until your dedicated session, using time blocks properly, and avoiding distractions.

You can also do a mental dump, consciously setting aside things you know you'll never get done (nice-to-do items with little impact).

Just as being tidy with your thoughts (your mental filing system) helps you function effectively, so does keeping your working area clear. You can get so used to clutter that you don't realise it's intruding. Try to touch each piece of paper as few times as possible, ideally only once or twice.

I feel hemmed in mentally if I have a messy desk. A good clear out clears my head; it's liberating and it allows me to focus on the important tasks. Nowadays I don't let it get so bad; besides, it's easier to find information when it's filed away or stored digitally.

What about emails that come after you subscribe to get a freebie? Have they outlived their usefulness? Decide which to keep (I hope my School Financial Success newsletter is among them!) and click the unsubscribe button on the rest.

You might think you don't have room in your busy day to sort through your clutter, but the effort is worth it in the long run. After a major session, you'll realise keeping it tidy as you go along is best.

James Clear, the author of 'Atomic Habits' (link), believes tiny habits are part of a larger system for creating remarkable results. He says the Four Laws of Behaviour Change are to make your habits obvious, attractive, easy and satisfying.

Identify a habit you'd like to develop and consider how you can make it fit the following descriptions:

1. **Obvious.** Scheduling it at the same time every day makes it more memorable. Set an alarm, and put a Please Do Not Disturb notice on your door or desk; I've even heard of people who put on a hat as a signal that they can't be interrupted!

2. **Attractive.** Link it to something you enjoy. Listen to your favourite music on headphones. Have a cuppa or a treat, whatever you prefer.

3. **Easy.** Don't set unrealistic targets, like completing a whole flow chart or writing a full policy in one session. Set small goals you can easily reach; you may exceed them.

4. **Satisfying.** Besides seeing your plans progress, can you add another reward to motivate you to keep up the new

habit? Varying the reward can help, just as social media motivates us to keep scrolling by providing new posts.

Habit stacking

It doesn't take much concentration to make a cup of tea or coffee, or brush your teeth on a morning, does it? Use this regularity to introduce a new good habit as a follow on, for example doing some stretching or jogging on the spot while you're waiting for the kettle to boil. It works because you're using a current, regular and automatic cue to cultivate the new one. The less effort you need to make the cue happen, the easier it will be to embed the new habit.

By achieving a natural flow from one habit to the other, you'll create an automatic sequence. In no time at all, it will be easier to stick to the new one you've introduced. You'll end up with lots of micro-habits which will collectively bring a significant improvement in your well-being and productivity.

Activity 8 - Analysing habits

8.1 Make two lists of habits: ones which help you to be efficient and effective, and those that are holding you back.
8.2 How did you create the positive habits? Was it a conscious decision, and if so, how did you go about it?
8.3 Decide which negative habits you need to change. Jot down some ideas on how to stop them or replace them with helpful habits. Can you change the cue, routine or reward? How could you use the Four Laws of Behaviour Change and habit stacking to make it easier?

Key points

- To become more productive, we need to develop the right habits to make effective routines easier.
- Replacing negative habits with positive ones will help your mindset, improve your time management and give you more energy.
- Try to become aware of your habits and identify any that you need to change. Be patient; it takes time to stop or start them.
- Habits consist of a cue, a routine and a reward; use this knowledge to make changes. To introduce new ones successfully, try to make them obvious, attractive, easy and satisfying.
- Use habit stacking to create an automatic sequence of positive habits in every area of your life.

PART III

ORGANISE

Organise

Set the foundations

We are now moving up to stage two of our pyramid, taking practical steps to improve your productivity. It involves setting high-level goals and developing a plan of action. You'll discover how to use your time more productively, and try out lots of tips and techniques to save your energy and get things done efficiently.

In this part we'll be covering goal setting, moving from goals to a plan, being organised, setting boundaries and time management.

Are you ready? Great - let's dive in!

7

GOAL SETTING

The power of goals

As human beings, we need clarity and boundaries in our lives, and we achieve this by setting goals for ourselves. They give us a sense of purpose, motivating us to organise ourselves so we can achieve them. They are essential for productivity; when making a journey, we need to know where we're headed before we decide how to get there.

You may already have a clear set of life goals; if so, use this chapter to reflect on whether you want to change, delete or add any. If you haven't set goals, this is your opportunity to try. I'll be guiding you through the process of identifying a long-list, then narrowing this down and getting a sense of which are the most important.

Clear goals help us to direct our thoughts to what we want to achieve. Your brain can be selective in what it gives attention to or ignores; it's trying to find patterns, making a connection with your recent decisions. It's your job to steer it towards what's important.

If your focus and thoughts are all about the things you want to do and who you want to be, it's more likely than not that you'll achieve them. I started planning for early retirement around 2-3 years in advance, after some friendly nagging from our HR lead. I joined an

Additional Voluntary Contributions (AVC) scheme and put aside as much money as possible from my salary each month. The beauty of this scheme is that the tax relief on the payment is added to the pot; free money from HMRC is always welcome! It provided an extra lump sum when I retired at 55, partly making up for the reduction in pension. For me, it was about freedom of choice in how I wanted to live.

Visualisation is a technique used by high achievers; it places a positive aspiration in your brain. Your subconscious then looks for opportunities to make it happen. So why not take advantage of this and do it deliberately?

Olympic athlete Sally Gunnell OBE gave a motivational speech at a Schools North East conference in 2018. She described how she prepared for the Olympics by visualising herself running the race of her life, imagining every stage of it all going exactly to plan, to win her gold medal. Her talk can be viewed on YouTube (link).

You can apply this technique in any area of your life. Creating a vivid mental image of your ideal situation will motivate you to make it happen. But try to keep it realistic; if you imagine yourself sipping cocktails on a millionaire's yacht or being selected to play for England in whatever sport you enjoy, you'll only end up dissatisfied!

Follow the best people

Another well-known assertion is that the five people you spend the most time with will determine the sort of person you'll become. Your brain absorbs all the messages it picks up and you find yourself adopting the same attitude and behaviours. If this is true, then it makes sense to take a conscious decision about who to follow.

When I was planning to become a freelancer, it was daunting. Since leaving university, I'd always had an employer. There were lots of risks to self-employment, and many new skills to learn such as website creation, marketing, and indie publishing.

Once I knew what success would look like for me, I identified the type of people I wanted to be around. They were my self-appointed informal mentors, much as you might watch an outstanding leader to understand how to improve your management skills. I chose industry experts, learned to identify best practice, connected with various people on social media platforms and met some of them in person at top quality conferences and workshops. Gradually, I absorbed all the tips and techniques, and now I can pay it forward by helping others.

Without this clarity of purpose, we are more likely to drift along, not achieving anything in particular, left to the mercy of others who may try to manipulate us for their own purposes.

A school outlines its purpose and objectives in a school development plan, and it should align the job descriptions for every member of staff with it. Everything needs to fit together, with a 'golden thread' running from the vision to everyday operations.

But do you have a personal plan, where you set out your life goals and the things you must change to achieve them? I'm not suggesting you need to write it in blood or that you'll be a failure if you don't achieve it. Think of it as a set of guideposts. You are more important than your job, more than just a post holder.

Our lives are complex, made up of so many areas: family and friends, intimate relationships, career, money, health, leisure pursuits, and our environment. Imagine achieving your ideal balance in life. Does it feel good? To make it happen, create goals which will help you become the person you want to be in the other aspects of your life too. I'd encourage you to think about all these areas when you're considering the tips and techniques in this book for saving time and being better organised.

The best goals stretch us, provide a challenge and are satisfying to achieve. So let's look at how to start creating and refining them for both personal and professional success.

Your definition of success

Who do you want to be? What do you want to be remembered for? These are big questions, but you'd be surprised how many people can't give me an answer when I ask this. I don't leap on innocent people in the street and pin them to the wall with a barrage of questions, you understand; I'm talking about when I've mentored people or had tricky conversations about performance in organisations.

What is your definition of success? More responsibility, more money, respect, recognition, or simply the satisfaction of a job well done at the end of the month? We all have dreams, but for them to have any chance of happening, we need to turn them into a goal.

What's the difference, I hear you ask? Well, a dream just sits there and occasionally we sigh and think of it. Mine is to spend every winter living in a warmer country. My husband has retired, and I've set up my life so I can work from anywhere writing books and blog posts, copy-editing for other authors and producing online courses, so technically it's possible, as long as I have access to the internet.

But it's a fairly unrealistic dream. We have three (supposedly grown-up) children and three gorgeous granddaughters. I'd miss them too much, and we always seem to be rushing to their aid.

A goal, on the other hand, is something we are actively working towards. We know what needs to be done to achieve it and we are formulating plans to carry out those actions, hopefully with a timeline, a regular review and adjustments to make sure we keep on track.

Going deeper: your 'Why'

To create meaningful goals, it's helpful to be clear not only about our definition of outward success, but also our internal reasons for wanting it.

Yet how many of us stop and work this out? Time goes by so quickly and we get immersed in the minutiae of the days, which rapidly turn into weeks and months, unless you're waiting for a holiday, of course, in which case time has a habit of dragging its heels.

Start by asking yourself a couple of relatively easy questions (easy as in there's no wrong answer). Was there a particular reason you were attracted to a career in education, and why did you choose school business management?

My reason for spending my career in education is very personal. School was my oasis during a difficult childhood, after my dad left home when I was ten. I spent as much time at school as I could, as a member of the orchestra, choir, Debating Society and Gilbert & Sullivan Society. Our Latin teacher took a group of us to archaeological sites at weekends, in a battered old van with benches in the back which would never pass health and safety criteria today. I enjoyed guide camp too, where we all travelled in the back of a removals van, sitting among the camping equipment with only a half tail door to stop us falling out, singing at the top of our voices as we went along. Guess what? We survived.

Sorry, I digress! Anyway, my English teacher suggested I should go to university. 'What's university?' I asked. I went, and it made a world of difference to me. This is at the heart of my passion for education. It helped me out of poverty and gave me a terrific career.

My 'Why' is a determination that all children should have the opportunities to be the best they can be, just as I did. My mission in setting up School Financial Success was to use my skills to help others to give children a chance. I provide a lot of information free, hoping it will guide school leaders to use resources wisely.

Your reason doesn't have to be deep seated; many people fall into professions by accident. It doesn't have to be grand or emotional. But there will probably be a reason why you've stuck with it.

Activity 9 - What is your 'Why'?

9.1 Write in your workbook for at least ten minutes about why you do what you do.
9.2 Think of all the people, events and situations which have shaped your decisions.
• What is it about your nature, your aptitude and abilities, that make this career a good fit for you?
• What attracted you to your current job?
• What led to your choice of this school or previous places where you were given opportunities to grow your skills?

9.3 Find the best statement among your writing which sums up your 'Why', and make a poster out of it, either by hand or using the free tool at Canva.com to create a background image and attractive text. Stick it on your wall; when things get difficult, you'll have a visual reminder of why you're doing all this.

Who do you want to be?

Understanding your 'why' leads you to the next question: who do you want to be in the future? What does success look like for you?

You can reflect on this for various stages of your life. When you leave this job, what do you want to have achieved? What would you like people to say at your leaving presentation? It doesn't do any harm to think about how you'd like to be thought of at the end of your career. It can guide your actions and behaviours.

This visioning exercise is a great way to achieve clarity on how you want to spend the next phase of your working life. There's not much point if a goal takes you in the opposite direction to what you want to do or be; that will only cause frustration and regrets.

Having a vision for the future helps you to be more intentional about achieving your hopes and dreams. It makes it easier to identify areas where you need to develop your skills and knowledge, and to spot the barriers which are holding you back.

Activity 10 - Who do you want to be?

10.1 In your workbook, jot down your thoughts on what sort of person you want to be, and what success would mean to you.
You will find some useful prompts in the workbook.
Soon, you'll be using these notes to spark ideas for your goals.

Strategic goals

Strategic goals are ambitious and inspiring, and usually long-term. They should provide a strong motivation for what you do. The principles on which they're founded are unlikely to change; it's the tactics you employ that will need some flexibility, so you can respond to changing circumstances around you.

As an example, when I realised I wanted to change my working life, my strategic goals were to become a freelance consultant and a published writer, and to have the freedom to explore new places in the UK and abroad whenever I wanted.

Initially, you can come up with as many as you like; you'll be narrowing them down later. The important thing is to distinguish the strategic from the operational. You might have a burning desire to find out where the caretaker disappears off to when you need him or her, or to discover why your school gets through glue sticks faster than the nation consumes chocolate digestives, but they're definitely operational matters.

A strategic goal might be to create a sustainable budget for the medium term for your school, but setting the annual budget and closing the accounts would be operational objectives. Developing a MAT-wide procurement strategy with a plan to streamline it at the trust level is strategic, but letting a series of contracts is operational. Your scope of responsibility and examples may be different.

Don't be afraid to think big; ambitions come from our strongest desires. Mine come from my childhood desire to be in control, to have freedom and choice. I wanted to return to my first love of school finance and funding, instead of working across so many disciplines.

We often place limits on our own ambitions. This can be down to imposter syndrome, the belief that we struck lucky when we got the job, it was a fluke, we don't deserve it, or we'll be found out. Why do we torture ourselves with these fears? In my experience, those who feel this way are more likely to be good at what they do, because they care. The people who are less effective are usually those who are full of bluff and bluster, letting everyone know how important they are!

At this stage you're simply identifying a long-list of potential goals. Don't be tempted to run before you can walk; you don't need to start planning how to make them happen yet. All in good time.

Coming up with goals

It's natural to have different goals for different stages of your life, like stepping stones across a river (but they won't always be in a nice straight line). If you have caring responsibilities, your focus is bound to be more immediate, and it might be difficult to think far ahead. But try to take a helicopter view and consider where you want to be in the long term. It gives you something to aim for. When you're struggling, goals can spur you on, because you have a path to something better.

Check your goals suit your beliefs and your values. You'll be working hard on them, and you don't want to find out later that you've chosen the wrong ones. A later chapter looks at what to do if there isn't a good match between you and your school's ethos.

Your personal goals are your own, so you have free rein with them. But your current professional goals should fit with your school's vision and objectives, to fulfil your job description. Are you clinging on to any past goals which are no longer relevant or desirable? Be honest: are there some you will never achieve because you have no intention of doing what it takes to make them happen? It's time to do a Marie Kondo-style clear-out and keep them sharp and minimalist. You may not be able to choose all of your work-related ones, but you can make sure your personal ones are those that matter the most to you and will 'spark joy'.

Identifying your strategic goals

Now for our next activity, which uses sticky notes. You know the type I mean, P-Its, but authors have to be careful about mentioning trademarks, so I'm using the term 'sticky notes' from now on. Their big advantage is disposability; they encourage you to play with ideas, because you don't feel you're committing to anything permanent.

I use sticky notes whenever I need to generate ideas. This book started off life as a set of sticky notes for the main topics, which I arranged on separate sheets, adding sub-headings. I then moved them around until I was happy with the initial structure.

By the way, if you'll allow a short digression, I must share a secret about sticky notes. You know how they curl up and fall off the wall? Well, you're probably peeling them from the bottom up. Try peeling them from the short side of the sticky band, and you'll find they lie flat. Honestly, try it and see! Cheaper brands can still be problematic though. If that's not a transformational tip, I don't know what is.

Activity 11 - Your strategic goals

You'll be using your notes from activities 9 and 10 in this exercise, and you'll also need a pack of sticky notes.
11.1 Scribble down any big goals which come to mind, both personal and professional, one per sticky note.
11.2 Check they will take you closer to who you want to be, and that they are consistent with your purpose, your 'Why'.
11.3 Try to imagine yourself in five or even ten years' time. What could be different if you achieve your goals?
11.4 Keep the sticky notes, as you'll need them for a future activity.

The possibilities are endless, limited only by your imagination, so find a place where you can relax and let your subconscious mind bring up ideas. Free writing is effective for this sort of exercise.

Reflection
When you've run out of ideas, stand back and look at them. How different are they from any you've set in the past? What does this suggest about your future potential?

Now look for any themes. Are some of them similar in intent? Group them together. Write down your list of goals in your workbook; we'll be returning to them soon.

Review work-related goals

Some of your strategic goals may be a given, by virtue of your position in school; you won't have a free choice in them. Are you fully invested in them, or do you believe they don't reflect what you do? Are they sharp enough to ensure the organisation moves forward and secures continuous improvement?

There's nothing worse than striving to achieve the wrong goals. It's disheartening and a waste of your valuable time. So it's a good idea to take a step back and look at them. I'm sure your leader wouldn't want you spending hours on tasks with low impact.

Activity 12 - Review of work-related goals

12.1 Consider the list you compiled in Activity 11 and put a mark against any which have to be there because of your current job. Add any big goals you have missed.
12.2 Ask yourself a series of questions to check if they're appropriate and deliverable. Here are some prompts, but feel free to add your own:
• Are they the right goals to deliver what the organisation needs?
• Do you have a fair chance of achieving them?
• Are the timescales realistic, given the work involved?
• What measures will be used to assess your progress and achievement?

• Are your success measures relevant, transparent, fair and easily quantified?

12.3 Record your thoughts in the workbook pages for this activity.

Reflection

Look at your notes. Has this review of your proposed goals unearthed any problems? Has it highlighted any reasons why you're struggling to be productive or show impact in what you're doing?

———

Your findings could prompt you to ask your manager for a conversation about workload and well-being. Raising it isn't an admission of failure; you are giving your employer a chance to hold on to a good member of staff by carrying out their duty of care to you.

If you're still hesitating about raising the subject, look at it from your manager's point of view. I'd want to know if any member of my staff was struggling through no fault of their own, and I'd be keen to see how we could make things right. The upheaval and cost of losing a valued member of the team, advertising, recruiting and training a new person doesn't bear thinking about, compared to a few adjustments to keep an SBP who would be happier and more productive.

Identify your priority goals

You will need to place a limit on how many strategic goals you are going to pursue. If you identify too many, it will be much harder to achieve them all within the timescales you or anyone else has set. The most effective people focus on a few big goals, which gives them a far higher chance of success than a scattergun approach.

So, identifying your priority goals is one of the most important things you can do to be more productive. They may take time to bear fruit, but the rewards are greater. It's also beneficial to have some smaller ones to provide quick wins, create impetus and motivate you.

Now you have your longlist of goals, you need to look at them all with a more dispassionate eye, to consider whether they are essential and identify their order of importance. Here are a couple of ways to think about them before you dive into the activity.

Your life as a jar

Have you come across the metaphor of your life being like a big jar which you're filling with all the things you have to do? No one seems to know where it originated, but it's a useful visual image to consider how you are allocating your time.

Imagine a very large jar. Now picture three bowls, one full of large rocks, one with smaller rocks and pebbles, and one full of sand. If you put the sand in the jar first, then the pebbles, there won't be room for all the rocks. But if you do it the opposite way round, you'll fit in all the rocks and pebbles, and the sand will still find a way in.

Your priority goals are big rocks, and the rest are smaller rocks and pebbles. The little routine jobs which take up a lot of time each day are grains of sand. You can't avoid the sand; it still has to be fitted in to the jar, but it will need to wait in line.

This is why understanding your priorities is so vital. I'll be referring to the 'life jar' again in the next chapter when you start converting your goals into actions. What you need to do next is make sure you have the right 'big rocks' to work on: your priority goals.

Pyramid of priorities

Creative coach Dan Blank (link) suggests a technique called 'Clarity Cards' which I have used this year to identify the most important goals I want to focus on. My version of it here is meant to help you prioritise the goals you've already decided on. I call it a 'Pyramid of Priorities'.

Activity 13 - Prioritise your goals

13.1 Return to your sticky notes from Activity 11.

13.2 Arrange the notes in a pyramid shape, with one at the top level, two at the next, then three, four and so on. Place those which matter most to you at the top, then work across and down. They're all important, so think about the relativity between them. The workbook provides some prompts.

13.3 Play with them until you're happy with the order; you might suddenly realise one of them is a burning desire.

13.4 If you have more than three rows, remove those below the third row and put them to one side. Double check the six remaining items; these are your top priorities. Some of the discarded items (medium-sized rocks and pebbles) can still be fitted in with good organisation but the top six are the vital ones.

13.5 Take a photo and stick it in your workbook (or draw the pyramid) to record it for future reference.

You don't have to have as many as six goals; go with what suits you. However, more than six suggests they aren't strategic enough. If they are, you might struggle to attain them all. The whole point is to avoid being overwhelmed.

Reflection

What do your choices mean for the new balance you're trying to create? What will you be doing differently if you follow this path? Will it feel right?

Look at the discarded items. Do you need to give up any of them? How different will removing them make you feel? The energy released can be channelled into the priority goals. You might have a sense of guilt at letting some people down, but the time it frees up will be liberating and could let you help more people in the long run.

You will soon be breaking down each of the individual cards into smaller projects or work streams. Always remember to leave room for your top priority goals.

Key points

- Goals are powerful; they give us clarity, boundaries, and a sense of purpose, motivating us to organise ourselves to realise them.
- Using techniques like visualisation and identifying the best people to follow will give you a clarity of purpose.
- What's your definition of success? Use this to identify the goals you want to work towards.
- What's your 'Why'? How did you choose this career, this school, this life? And who do you want to be in the future? Knowing is the first step to achieving it.
- Make your goals big and strategic. Get all your ideas out, reflect on emerging themes, then identify a manageable number, personal and professional, which reflect your beliefs and values.
- Review your work-related items. Check they're right for you and your school, and don't be afraid to talk to your leader if you identify any issues.
- Identify your life jar 'big rocks' by using the Pyramid of Priorities approach (up to six). Reflect on what your choices mean for the new balance you're trying to create.

8
___

FROM GOALS TO A PLAN

Break down your goals

You've done well to develop your initial ideas into a set of strategic goals. Now you'll be eager to make a start on the activities that will help you achieve them.

In 'The 7 Habits of Highly Effective People' (link), Stephen R. Covey says the most successful people are more likely to start with the end in mind. They align their actions with their goals.

Breaking things down helps you cope better. Your brain feels less stressed dealing with smaller tasks because it doesn't have to make as many connections. Less time worrying means more time for action and you get more satisfaction as smaller tasks are completed, which keeps you motivated.

So, you're now going to break down your priority goals (your big rocks), setting out the steps involved and the order in which they should be completed. Identifying timescales and resources will come later. You don't have to start from scratch; you can align your current plans with the new goals. If some don't fit, can you eliminate them? Keep it simple and bring everything under the same umbrella.

I'd advise you to work on your priority goals first. Don't spend time on the lesser ones, only to discover there's no room for them.

Activity 14 - Break down your priority goals

You'll need a flip chart pad, a pen and sticky notes in several colours (yay!).
14.1 Write the first priority goal from Activity 13 on a sticky note and put it at the centre of a piece of flip chart paper.
14.2 Write down each step you need to take to achieve it, one per sticky note, and add them to the paper. Summarise large projects in a few sticky notes; you can divide them up later.
14.3 Work quickly and let the ideas flow. Don't stop and don't judge; write down whatever emerges.
14.4 Repeat the process for the other priority goals in different colours on individual flip chart pages.
14.5 Consult your current To Do list for any extra items.
14.6 Take a photo of your final results for future reference.
14.7 Create a planning document and transfer the steps into it, arranging them under each goal in a logical order with a clear description. This will form the start of your new work plan.
Keep the sticky notes; you'll be re-using them soon.

Reflection

Review the steps under each priority goal in your planning document. Do you need to rearrange any of the items, group them differently or change the sequence?

There is space in the workbook to add helpful notes. You might want to sketch out the parts of a project, plot inter-dependencies or work out a sequence.

An example might be helpful. Imagine one of your goals is a big increase in additional funds for your school or trust by developing an income generation strategy (the topic of my first online course).

On my 'psbp-links' webpage (link), I've provided a photo of my sticky note activity results, showing the steps to produce an Income Generation Strategy. I've grouped the more detailed ideas to save space; they would normally be separate sticky notes.

You should now be able to tell whether there's room for any 'small rocks', or whether you're over-committing yourself with your top priorities. Amend your plan as necessary.

I expect you'll be eager to start adding timelines, resources and responsibilities. But as a productivity check, I'd like you to pause first and review your assumptions about who should complete the work.

Don't fall into the trap of assuming you have to do it all. I have two techniques for you to use to assess this.

Important and urgent tasks

The art of being organised hinges on exercising control over what you spend time on. Forward planning can help, whether it's identifying your priority goals, understanding the tasks within them, or deciding which tasks you'll do tomorrow.

Being busy can be addictive. It validates us and makes us feel we're achieving something. But is what you're doing worth spending your valuable time on? Will you see tangible results? Here's a technique to help you decide if you're the right person to do a task.

Important/urgent analysis

In a 1954 speech, former U.S. President Dwight D. Eisenhower said: 'I have two kinds of problems: the urgent and the important. The urgent are not important, and the important are never urgent.' This has become known as the 'Eisenhower Principle'. It's explained in an article on the Mindtools website (link) and it is a commonly used approach in planning for productivity.

If you aren't clear about what's important and what isn't, your tendency will be to gravitate towards the urgent, because you sense there'll be trouble if you don't complete it. You probably won't stop to consider whether or not an urgent task is important. By acting in this way, you're allowing others to control your workload.

If you can spot tasks which have been perceived as urgent by someone else, you can question whether you have to do them now, or whether you can delay them or delegate them to others.

However, you won't be able to avoid urgent demands completely; some are completely unforeseen. So, when planning your schedule, build in some leeway for genuinely urgent items. You can't predict when they'll arise, so you need some flexibility to cope with them.

You've probably heard of or may already be using the important/urgent matrix (The Eisenhower Matrix) to separate essential tasks from those which others regard as urgent but which will distract you from your own vital work. The horizontal X-axis represents the level of urgency, with the left-hand side being the most urgent and the right-hand side the least. The vertical Y-axis represents importance, with the lowest importance at the bottom and the highest at the top.

	Urgent	Not urgent
Important	1 DO	2 PLAN
Not important	3 DELEGATE	4 ELIMINATE

You can create your own version of the matrix and plot your tasks on it. What will happen to you, and to other staff, pupils and the school if you don't do them? The more serious the consequences, the higher the important and urgent rating will be.

You could keep a version of the matrix on your wall to remind you to triage each request, as a nurse in Accident & Emergency would, and decide which quadrant it fits into. It will help you retain more control over how you spend your time.

Quadrant 1 tasks are your first port of call when planning your day. But make sure you are the only one who can do them. Completing them early provides a sense of achievement, and the inevitable interruptions during the day won't induce as much panic.

Quadrant 2 tasks are still important but can be allocated to an appropriate slot in your schedule when your energy is highest and you can find a quiet place to work. You can identify interdependencies and check you have all the information before completing them.

Quadrant 3, delegation, can be difficult if you like to be in control, or if you don't trust anyone else to do the tasks as effectively as you could (in which case I'll politely ask you to challenge those assumptions). If you don't have a team, it's even harder, because you'll need to persuade your leader either to identify some other sources of support or to accept you can't fit them in and move them to quadrant 4.

Changing your mindset can help with delegation. These tasks are of lesser importance, so it's a safe space to test out your colleagues' ability and check progress from a distance.

Quadrant 4, the Eliminate option, can be difficult, especially for completer-finishers in the Belbin Team Roles analysis (link). But it is essential for your sanity, so you have to be ruthless. I bet these items will never get done anyway, so why let them sit there making you stressed? Set a timer and go through your list crossing out items of limited use and feel the weight lifting from your shoulders. If you're still struggling with the concept, put them on a Not To Do list and hide it!

In chapter 10, Set Boundaries, I'll talk more about how to delegate and eliminate items from your list. For now, consider discussing tasks in quadrants 3 and 4 with your manager.

As well as deciding on the relative order of the tasks under your priority goals, the next activity will help you reduce the size of your existing To Do list. This is your chance to sort it out and bring everything together before embarking on your sparkly new approach.

Activity 15 - Your Important/Urgent matrix

15.1 Create an Important/Urgent matrix on a large sheet of paper and plot the sticky notes from Activity 14 on it. You might need to break down some of them into individual notes if they fall into different quadrants. Think about the relative importance and urgency of each item to the rest.

15.2 Review the chart and move the sticky notes around until you're happy with the results.

15.3 In your planning document, mark the quadrant number against each of the items in a separate column. This will allow you to sort them by quadrant number if desired.

15.4 For items in quadrant 4, either remove them from your planning document or add the necessary action to allow you to eliminate them.

Frequent/complex analysis

Another way of classifying activities, which may work well for SBPs, is to understand the frequency and complexity of tasks. It will help you decide whether you are the right person to do them, when to schedule them, and what sort of energy is needed to complete them.

Frequency

You can divide tasks into three frequency categories. The first is for regular routines which you do every day, week or month. These form your bread and butter work, mainly operational tasks. They are instinctive, but please have a procedures manual, in case you leave!

The second category will be less frequent: half-termly, termly and annual. Many will be predictable, such as budget setting, closure of accounts or statutory returns. Others are less predictable, although I have detected a trend of important DfE announcements appearing on the last day of every term!

Pay particular attention to infrequent tasks with important deadlines; you may need to re-acquaint yourself with what's needed, and they invariably monopolise your time as the deadline approaches, causing other work to pile up. Can you pass anything to others?

The third category relates to one-off items: responses to emergencies like Coronavirus (hopefully it's a one-off), or a non-recurring project. You'll want to re-order your priorities once the crisis is over.

Look at the balance between your ongoing and irregular tasks. Too much in the ongoing list is a warning sign. You need capacity to do big and important projects. If you end up with a backlog, treat it like a project, adopting the little and often approach.

Tasks which are linked to events should ideally be spread throughout the year. The adrenaline rush from being under pressure to perform is stimulating, not harmful, when it's for a limited amount of time. Stress occurs when stimulation goes on for too long, so you need recovery space in between intense activities.

Your overall aim should be to create a better balance. Review your scheduling; identify jobs with more flexible timescales which can be moved around, like policy reviews.

Complexity

The energy levels required for some types of work are linked to the complexity of the task. You need extended time for some projects, especially those which have lots of interdependencies, need substantial research, and/or have to be wrestled into something non-specialists will understand, in order to get the decision you want.

If you're trying to follow government guidance, the language might be inaccessible or difficult to apply to your situation. There could be conflicting interpretations of the information, which need to be resolved before you can make progress. The list goes on; these are all things I've had to overcome in the past, and I imagine you can come up with lots of examples too.

I explain more about this in other chapters, but for now my point is that you'll do better spending big chunks of time on complex tasks.

Avoid scheduling too many minor tasks on days when you are doing complex work. It's better to batch smaller, easier tasks together on a day when your brain needs a break from intensive thinking.

Schedule your tasks

You should now have a better idea of the tasks which only you can do (quadrants 1 and 2) and the necessary actions to delegate and eliminate other tasks (quadrants 3 and 4). These details will form the skeleton of your planning document. Now you can develop your schedule by adding timelines to keep you moving towards your goals. Accept the inevitability that other things will emerge. Use the important/urgent matrix to triage them: do you need to slot them into your plan, and if so, where should they sit?

Think about the rhythm of the year and use it to allocate your priority tasks into time slots. Start off with annual and termly blocks, then break these down into shorter periods, depending on the nature and frequency of the tasks.

As you work on your plan, you'll come across larger projects which need to be broken down further. Start from the completion date and work backwards to allocate sufficient time to them.

Be aware of the most demanding times for colleagues on whom you rely to provide information, especially where you have a tight deadline. You don't want to be stuck waiting for an important set of data or for someone else to take a decision before you can complete your part of it. Lead-in times for procurement exercises are a particularly challenging example. You will be reliant on a range of people for individual steps, and the processes have to be observed carefully to avoid legal challenges.

Your planning schedule is not meant to be set in stone; it's a framework. You need a degree of flexibility, because unexpected things happen (as we know from the Covid-19 pandemic). I set aside time on a Sunday evening to allocate my planned work across the next five days. If I schedule it too far in advance, I know I'll end up making a lot of changes as other tasks emerge. Keep referring to your bigger blocks of monthly and weekly tasks to monitor your progress and check they're still the right ones to support your goals.

Measure success

Do you finish a project or a task and then move straight on to the next one? I know I do. There's so much to be done that we never seem to stop and celebrate an achievement. But we all need a bit of encouragement, so even if no one else thinks it's important, you should take a moment to congratulate yourself for finishing a piece of work.

How will you know you've succeeded? We've already seen that creating your own definition of success gives you something firm to aim at. But it also helps to have visible way markers at various points along the way, even for relatively small goals.

Do you have a means of tracking your progress which you can see on a day-to-day basis, as a reminder of the progress you've made? It can be as simple as a list on a noticeboard, or a note in a phone app which you consult regularly. But don't delete the task when it's completed; you need a way of marking it as done. This will motivate you, and it makes you accountable to yourself.

Here's a tip: don't feel a failure if you haven't been able to tick off everything. There will be reasons; something else more important might have cropped up, or maybe some of the items shouldn't have been on the list because they're not urgent. You can justifiably carry forward non-urgent tasks to the next week or month without the sky falling in. It's a good test of what's essential.

Let's look at some approaches you can use for this stage of breaking down your tasks. The next section is like a pick and mix sweet stand; try something and see if it works for you. If it doesn't suit, tweak it or try something else.

My planning system

What tools do you use to turn your goals into tasks and monitor your progress? I thought you might like to know how I do it. But be warned; I love planning. It makes me feel as if I'm halfway there!

I start by sketching out my big goals for the year on sticky notes, and I mull over them for a few days before doing my pyramid of priorities. I balance the most important ones across the year by allocating them to quarters, in an attempt to avoid overloading myself (cue hollow laughter). I make allowances for holidays and the rhythm of my consultancy, which tends to match the LA and school budgeting cycle.

Then I break them all down using Trello (link), a project management app which sits in the cloud, synchronising the content across all your devices. It works on a tiered basis: boards for all your projects, lists within a project and cards within a list. There's lots of functionality such as checklists, due dates, attachments, and collaboration tools.

Trello is free, so why not have a play?

Productivity planners

As each quarter approaches, I break down my goals across the next three months, incorporating information from Trello for bigger projects.

Once I have the whole picture of each quarter and the three months within it, I turn to my Productivity Planners, which are free to download month by month from the Productive Flourishing Planners page (link). I use them to schedule my tasks across the months and weeks.

The monthly and weekly planners allow me to record quarterly, monthly and weekly objectives, and break down the weekly tasks into days. I can tick them off as complete and record my estimated and actual time spent. You can view the formats at the link I've provided.

Every morning I consult my weekly planner to remind me what I need to accomplish that day, and at some point in the afternoon I'll mark off what I've completed and check I'm on track for the remaining tasks.

There are also daily planners which allow you to allocate tasks across the day, but I find them too detailed. I tailor my work to my energy levels and alertness, so assigning rigid times wouldn't work for me. Instead, I write detailed daily tasks in my day-to-a-page academic year diary (more stationery is always good, right?), with room to add new items, notes, and reminders.

I like to print my planners; I fill them in by hand and keep them in a folder. But you can buy a cheap digital version covering the whole year, or a printed and bound version with a free Momentum Planning e-course; the website blog is also worth a read. The important thing is finding a way that works for you. A friend uses a bullet journal system, but I haven't investigated that yet.

My other important item is a whiteboard, on which I record my top-level monthly tasks. I keep it in a visible place as a silent motivator! I enjoy marking each item as completed; at the end of the month I take a photograph of it and store it in a Productivity folder on Dropbox. Whenever I am being self-critical for not getting enough done, I look back at the photos to see how much I've accomplished.

Alternative approaches

There are plenty of other options, and your school may already have systems which work well. Nikola Flint, my co-author for earlier books, shared her experience of Microsoft To Do with me:

'I have a series of To Do lists on my phone that I can share with other people. Anyone in the group can add tasks, allocate them to individuals in the group, add a detailed progress update, or upload evidence including photos, documents or spreadsheets. I use it to structure my progress meetings but it is a constant communication tool. I can't remember life without it; it's amazing. You can also keep your own individual To Do Lists in the same place if you choose to, both professional and personal.'

Activity 16 - Your planning system

16.1 Write some notes on how you currently record your goals and track your progress. What works for you, and are there any aspects which aren't as effective? Does it help you schedule tasks at the right times, ensure nothing is missed, and motivate you? How could your system be improved?

16.2 Decide what combination of systems you will use in the future. Record in your workbook what you intend to do and how it will make you more productive.

16.3 Test out your ideas for a trial period.

16.4 After your trial, come back to your workbook, re-read your notes and decide whether you've achieved what you intended. Make some notes on how it went; tweak it for another trial period if needed.

Key points

- Starting with the end in mind and aligning your actions with your goals will help you be more productive.
- Break down your priority goals, identifying the steps you need to take. Create a planning document for success.
- Use the Important/Urgent matrix to organise and flag your tasks in your work plan.
- Use the Frequent/Complex analysis to schedule your work and set deadlines.
- Align your tasks with the rhythm of the year, allowing some flexibility for emerging projects.
- Identify success measures to track your progress.
- Create your own planning system to help you break down your goals and keep yourself accountable.

9

BE ORGANISED

Identify your commitments

You've identified the tasks needed to achieve your priority goals, but how do you balance them against all the unknowns: the requests and demands from everyone else? They can flood your day and leave you feeling as if you'll never get the important things done. It's like having multiple windows open in your browser and forcing your brain to pay attention to them all at the same time.

Happily, there are techniques to help you organise the individual detailed tasks which take up most of your day. They will reduce the time spent deciding what to do next, lowering your anxiety levels.

Here's one idea for you to try if it appeals; you can tailor it to suit your way of working. In his book 'Getting Things Done' (link), David Allen recommends five stages:

1. Capture: place anything which grabs your attention — commitments, ideas, tasks — into a collection tool or 'bucket'. Have as few buckets as possible, but as many as you need.
2. Clarify: process what it means. Is it actionable? If so,

decide what your next action is, or reclassify it as a project. If it's not essential, move it to a sometime/maybe list.

3. Organise: put it where it belongs, so you can tackle it at the appropriate time.
4. Reflect: set aside time to review all your buckets regularly.
5. Engage: do the tasks.

You can find out more at David Allen's website (link).

The benefit of this system is that once you've captured and stored all the detailed items waiting for your attention, your brain is free to focus on the current task. You're also less likely to forget something.

'Your mind is for having ideas, not holding them.' (David Allen)

You can decide what buckets to create. Here are Allen's examples:

- 'In' list - a place for every idea and every task. Once you've finished your focused work, do anything which will only take two minutes, then move the rest to other lists.
- 'Waiting' list - tasks you can't delegate and can't complete yet because you're waiting for someone else to act.
- 'Next Actions' list - tasks you can't delegate and must do next. If it needs multiple actions, put it on the Projects list.
- Projects list - more complex items with a series of actions.
- Some day/maybe list - things you'd like to do eventually.

The lists are dynamic; items move between them. You need to review them regularly to check everything's on the right list. Your buckets could be handwritten lists, apps on your phone, and a digital calendar with reminders for important deadlines and events. Reserve time slots for important pieces of work.

Once all your commitments are in the buckets, you can see whether a new task is important and decide if you can fit it in.

I don't use this system because I would probably spend more time on the lists than on my actions. One SBP told me they use colour coding to categorise their tasks on a single list. But the Getting It Done model, or aspects of it, may be suitable for you; it's always worth a try, and you can blend aspects of several models.

Get the important things done

Now you know which are your most important pieces of work, how do you make sure they get done? If you're anything like me, the list of what you believe you can accomplish in a day is far longer than what you can realistically complete.

How do you decide which items to do first from your list? Do you pounce on those you think are easier or more fun (a relative term!), rather than what's important? Some people like to clear small things first. I do sometimes, but not for too long. Rabbit-like, they multiply while I'm tackling the first set, and I fear I'll never get my big rocks in the jar. I prefer to use my early morning energy for intensive jobs which need my full concentration. Do whatever works for you.

On the assumption you've used the Important/Urgent matrix to remove Delegate and Eliminate items from your list, consider the items in quadrants 1 (Do) and 2 (Plan). You could place Now, Next, and Later flags on these in your To Do list, or colour code them. Make sure you've completed the quadrant 1 tasks (they're urgent, right?) before tackling any of the others.

Your 'Today' list

Productivity expert and creative coach Mark McGuinness, who has a productivity blog (link) recommends a tactic which I use to keep my Today list manageable and focus on my priority tasks. You won't be surprised to hear it involves the use of sticky notes!

1. Have one sticky note per day with today's essential tasks written on it. Choose the 3-inch square size, which forces you to limit the number. Around five per day is sensible.
2. If you have one big deadline to meet, don't add anything

else. Otherwise, put the most important task at the top, and apply your best energy to it.

3. If another task emerges, ask yourself if it's genuinely urgent. Do you have to do it today? If so, add it to the sticky note and estimate how long it will take.
4. If there isn't room for this new essential item, look at the others: can you spend less time on any of them? Could you cross off one of them and add it to tomorrow's sticky note?
5. If the new task doesn't have to be done today, add it to your generic To Do list. Don't do anything else with it now.

For this to work, you must regard today's list as closed; nothing can be added except sudden urgent demands which are out of your control. You need to make a reasonably accurate assessment of how long each task will take. Keep this under review and try to improve your time estimates, otherwise you'll never complete a daily list.

The principle behind this system is that if there is no space on the sticky note for an item, there's no space for it in your day. I recommend it if you're in overwhelm mode, because it challenges your thinking and makes your To Do list less threatening. You'll feel a sense of satisfaction in actually completing a To Do list. Never mind that it's a small list; the things on it were the most crucial tasks for today. How good does this feel? If you achieve them all with some time to spare (I know, we can all dream), there will be plenty of other things you can tackle.

As you read this, you're probably thinking your 43 tasks listed for today are all vitally important and you can't possibly choose just five. But remember this is about getting the most important things done, your big rocks, and we're taking one day at a time. It's all about balance. You're spreading the load in a manageable way so you can be confident of meeting deadlines, and you can see you're making progress. It will give you a boost when you look back and see how productive you've been.

Create quality time

A large project with lots of elements and/or a long time span can be daunting. Planning your approach will help you avoid panicking when the deadline is looming and you're miles from the finish line.

Quality time is crucial for these sorts of projects. You need to work on them regularly to be confident of hitting the deadline, because a lot of interdependencies bring a higher risk of delays. You may also need to keep others on track, depending on your role in the project.

If you don't have the luxury of long uninterrupted periods of time to devote to a project, scheduling regular 'little and often' sessions is the next best thing. Not only will it provide reassurance that you are on track, but you will spot potential problems early enough to do something about them. It also keeps the project in your mind, letting your subconscious mull over it while you do other work.

This approach has frequently been beneficial for me. If I've been faced with a knotty problem in the middle of a project, keeping it at the forefront of my mind has allowed ideas to emerge naturally, often when I'm out walking or doing something boring like ironing. This is why creating downtime is invaluable.

If you are struggling to make space for your project, why not make an arrangement with another person or team to take turns answering each other's phones for an hour or two on a regular basis? We did this in my local authority days, when teams needed uninterrupted time for in-house training or an urgent meeting.

You could mark off the days on a calendar to track when you've been active on a project. When writing my novel, I created a 'Don't break the writing chain' document and marked off numbered boxes for each day of writing. I could have put a daily word target on it, but I didn't want to obsess about the quantity and feel a failure if I couldn't sustain it. But you might find it helpful to put a measure on your routine, for example checking a number of budget lines per day for your next financial report. Do what works for you.

Key to my success was the vow not to break the chain. It's a common enough tactic to have a name: gamification. You create a competition with yourself or others. It uses our innate competitiveness as a motivator, something teachers often use with their classes. Think creatively about ways to create a competitive urge.

Timing

Timing is an important element in planning. How can you fit everything in? How about getting up earlier? Being in school before it gets busy allows you to concentrate better, which is invaluable for complex work where your brain needs space to spot patterns.

As ever, you need to adapt this to your own situation. For one thing, it depends on your family circumstances. For another, if your school has a lot of early birds, the office might not be quieter. Staying later might be better. This isn't about working extra hours. I hope you have the flexibility to adjust your start and finish times; enlightened leaders focus on what's achieved, not when and how it's done.

Understanding your energy levels is important. Late at night is not a productive time for me. It's far better if I wind down before bed, reading a book before I go to sleep. I naturally wake up early feeling fully refreshed and alert, and my work is done much more quickly and accurately, with far fewer revisions.

Report writing

Do you do a lot of report writing in your job? In my local authority career, I must have written hundreds of reports for officers, elected members and Schools Forums, so I had to become efficient at them.

Getting better at using Word was a key factor in speeding up my rate of production. Do you make full use of the Styles menu? You can create your own set of styles with various levels of headings, numbered paragraphs and bullet points. If you don't have a standard style in your school, create your own template; they're invaluable for all documents, not just reports. You'll spend less time fighting with the formatting in Word, which seems to have a mind of its own!

Outlining your reports in advance is another time saver. It helps you identify the key messages you want to get across, making your reports more succinct, easier for readers to digest, and hopefully more memorable. This is especially important if you're writing a persuasive report to get a favourable decision.

To build an outline, you can do a mind map to identify your key points, which will become your headings and sub-headings. If you haven't tried mind mapping before, there's a helpful five-minute video plus a TED talk by Tony Buzan, who invented it (link). I write my mind maps by hand, but you may prefer mind mapping software.

Whether you've prepared a mind map or a list, transfer your headings and sub-headings into your template report. Make sure it's in a logical order and you haven't missed anything. Then you can start to add in your main points in summary form.

Identify any research or figures you need to support your points. If you want to use tables, will they be in the body of the report or in appendices? You may already know the results of your analysis, but if you're starting afresh, consider tackling it first, to be clear about your main messages. Otherwise you may have to rework your narrative.

Now you can flesh out the points in more detail and add tables or diagrams, to produce your first draft.

You may want colleagues to write part of your report. Google Docs allows others to add comments or make changes. I suggest you draft a set of rules on what they can or can't change. You'll be able to see their contributions as you're working on it. It could also save you time and prevent frustration; copying other people's amendments into your master document can cause formatting problems.

It's a good idea to ask a trusted colleague to do a final read, because it's hard to spot your own errors, whether it's typos, illogical conclusions or omissions. If this isn't possible, try the Speak or Read Aloud function in Word. It can't cope with 'DfE' though; not being a scientist, it took me a while to figure out why it kept saying 'D iron'!

I like to save a report as a pdf and export it to my Kindle or Apple Books app on my iPad, and I always use a printed copy for my final read through. The magic of a different medium somehow makes it easier to spot errors. I'm in awe of how our brains work!

A sensible naming system for reports and appendices will save you from panicking when you need to find a document (which somehow only happens when it's urgent). Setting the footer to show the file name and location may be helpful if all you can find is a print copy. It's also worth reviewing your naming convention for folders. The location always makes sense when I'm saving a document, but when I need to find it, it's the last place I think of!

Is a report the right method for the information you want to communicate? Would a slide presentation be more effective at a meeting? How about an infographic (you can create it at Canva.com), where the data is conveyed in pictures and charts?

It's said we remember far more if we've been actively engaged in doing something rather than just sitting reading or listening, although personal preference also comes into it. So you could lead a mini-workshop, with questions designed to let your colleagues come up with solutions themselves, or develop your proposals further. There are many possibilities, so don't be afraid to think creatively about what your audience will find most thought-provoking and informative. It can boost your personal profile.

Record information

Do you take notes at meetings for future reference, to include in a report or a policy? For personal development, do you read books, blogs, take online courses, or visit websites?

How do you record all this information? What you do reach for when you hear or see something you want to capture: a notebook, your phone or something else? Try to design a system which is flexible enough and allows easy retrieval when needed. Your school will provide some systems, but think about all parts of your life.

Note taking is a skill you can develop. What you want to achieve by taking notes depends on the situation you're in. You won't normally need to make verbatim notes (unless you've been asked to take minutes, and if so, couldn't a less senior colleague do it?). You may want to record action points or pertinent information to help you take a decision or complete a task.

If you're in a meeting, focus on its purpose and the desired outcomes, and listen carefully for relevant noteworthy information. Learn to paraphrase, or use keywords which will trigger the full meaning when you re-read it. You might not be confident in this at first, but it will come with practice. Get into the habit of logging your action points as they emerge. I add new items to my ongoing To Do log in the back of my notebook immediately, then transfer them to the right place in my planning system.

Which style of note taking best suits you? Do you prefer a pictorial approach with diagrams, sketches, arrows and circles to make links between different points, or bulleted lists? How do you highlight actions, items to delegate and deadlines? Your approach may vary depending on whether the agenda includes reports which you can annotate, whether someone is writing on a flip chart which you can photograph with your phone, or whether they are presenting from a PowerPoint slide show which you will receive electronically.

Once you have a system you are comfortable with, you need to consider the best ways of retaining your notes. Let's look at a few different circumstances and examine some of the options available.

Learning

If I'm learning something, I know the information is more likely to stay in my brain if I write it by hand. This has been proven by science too. So if I'm reading a book, watching a webinar or listening to a podcast, I note down useful tips and action points. It's more relaxing for me to sit like this than use a device (or two if I'm watching on a laptop). I have a visual memory and can usually remember where the words are on a page. I often take a photo of an important note, in case I need it when my notebook isn't to hand.

But you may prefer a completely digital approach, using a tablet, phone or laptop and storing notes on cloud systems like Dropbox, iCloud, OneDrive, OneNote or Evernote. You can annotate books on

Kindle and export the notes via email, and you can save pdfs and other documents in Kindle or Apple Books for portability. It's all about what works for you.

Stationery Obsession Confession Time: I used to have several notebooks for different purposes. I could remember where on a page I wrote something, but not always which one it was in (I know, I'm odd). So now I have one master notebook for everything. It's pretty easy for me to recall when I was doing something, or consult my calendar app or my Sent emails. At the back, I keep my generic 'Inward To Do' log to capture all my commitments, then I transfer the most important items to my monthly whiteboard and my planners.

Notes from meetings

When I'm in meetings, I take notes on an iPad or my laptop; on my return, I synchronise the document to a Dropbox folder. Dropbox (link) is free for up to 2 GB of storage (or around £100 per year for 2 TB if you pay annually), and you can synchronise it between all your devices. I use it to back up all my files and photos. I can choose which folders to synchronise to each of my devices, so I only see those I'm currently working on, which saves a lot of space, but everything is accessible online.

Dropbox can be a life-saver, because deleted files and previous versions are accessible for up to 30 days after each change. You can share individual folders or files with others and send them a link.

You may have access to Apple iCloud or Microsoft OneDrive, which are similar. The important thing is having it backed up on the cloud rather than relying on your actual devices which might fail. Your office files should be backed up automatically, but what about your personal devices and information? It's still advisable to do a regular backup to a separate drive, in case the cloud system ever fails. You don't want the anxiety and effort of trying to recover files in the event of a major failure.

. . .

Alternative technologies

If you enjoy trying different approaches, keep an eye open for new technologies to aid productivity. Smartpens contain a camera, an audio recorder, and a built-in computer enabling users to record, save, and upload data. You can write by hand and transfer notes to your phone or tablet instantly. Two examples are the Livescribe Symphony and NeoLab N2 (links).

I've recently watched someone using a smart tablet called a Remarkable (link), which allows you to write by hand with a special pencil. It can convert your notes to text and save it as a document which you can send via email. It is also possible to draw diagrams and mind maps and save them as files. PDFs and books can be uploaded and annotated. Everything can be synchronised to other devices via Wi-Fi. It's reputed to feel more like writing on paper than other tablets. A plus for productivity is you can't access social media or email on it, so you are less likely to be distracted. There are various other products which are similar; happy hunting!

SBP Tamsin Moreton is a fan of an everlasting notebook (link):

'The Rocketbook is an example of one of the new 'everlasting' note-books now available. It's a helpful way to record notes during a meet-ing, as instead of typing them up afterwards, trying to remember where you wrote the notes and ensuring you have said notebook with you, you can scan the page using your smartphone. As well as being saved to the Rocketbook App, you can send to one of several pre-defined cloud destinations or just to your email address. The notebook is reusable, so once you have scanned the page you can wipe it clean to re-use.'

Saving webpages

You can tag a webpage as a favourite location on your computer, but what if you are away from it and can't remember the name? My solution to this is a free app called Pocket (link). You download an extension to your browser on all your devices, and whenever you want to save a URL, you click on the icon and add a tag. The online system is constantly updated when you have a connection, no matter which device you're on.

This has been a big time saver for my School Financial Success newsletter. Whenever I see an announcement, I save it and tag it as 'sfs newsletter'. Then when I'm producing the newsletter, I sign into the Pocket website, select the tag, and all my items are there ready to summarise in my mailing list software. You can attach multiple tags to a URL for different purposes, and you can edit or delete tags. I use Pocket for all my business and personal interests.

Tracking performance

Do you have a set of performance indicators to monitor? This is an area where electronic systems come into their own. Can you create a dashboard with all the key metrics in one place? This avoids having to open a host of different source files and collate everything manually. It may involve creating downloads to feed into an Excel spreadsheet with automatic updating of the links, or there may be better solutions within your own systems. A little research on how you can achieve this could conserve a lot of time and energy in the long run.

Templates

I've already mentioned using templates for reports, but you can break down any process to identify information which can be captured in a standard format. Templates can save time, achieve consistency, provide clarity on the standards expected, act as checklists, and give a professional impression both within and outside school.

Templates are especially efficient at collecting information from a range of people in a consistent format. This could include data to monitor performance across a trust-wide project, gathering requirements for a joint specification for a contract, or collating contextual data for a collaborative external funding bid with other schools.

Just imagine how much time it takes to fit everyone's facts into a standard format. It's just as quick for them to do the original work in a template as to write it free form, so why not save yourself the effort?

Other template-linked ideas

If you want to survey staff, pupils or parents, you can use ready-made templates like Google Forms or Survey Monkey web-based forms, which provide ready-made reports on the results.

Flow charts and infographics can be helpful in providing a pictorial representation of a process, so everyone can see the steps involved. Those who learn best visually might find them helpful.

Have you thought about making a training video to show staff how to operate a particular system or follow a process? You can record yourself talking over a demo using screen sharing within PowerPoint (on a Windows PC or laptop), Apple Keynote, Google Slides etc. Keep it simple and you'll avoid repeated explanations.

I'm assuming you already use cloud-based communications to make information available to people in your school community and beyond, but do you and your staff know how to get the most out of it? Watch out for resistance – some people believe knowledge is power and like to hold on to it themselves!

Activity 17 - Choose your shortcuts

17.1 Review the information in this chapter and make notes on how you can better organise your work.

17.2 Create a list of techniques and shortcuts to save time.

17.3 Make time to trial a selection over the next month.

17.4 At the end of the month, return to your workbook notes and record your findings.

17.5 Repeat with another set until you find the right balance.

Key points

- Organisation is the key to managing your time efficiently and effectively. Learn how to balance your priority goals against all the demands from other people.
- David Allen's 'Getting Things Done' method focuses on capturing every idea and task then deciding how to deal with them, organising them in lists based on actions.
- To set a more realistic target for your daily achievements, use a single sticky note per day with only your essential tasks on it. If there isn't room on the note for a task, there isn't room in your day.
- Create quality time for important projects, doing the work little and often to spot potential problems early and allow your subconscious the space to produce solutions. Use gamification tactics as motivation.
- Find pockets of time, try a different routine, and use your energy levels productively.
- Use templates, styles and outlining for a more efficient approach to report writing.
- Think about how you record and save information. Take advantage of technology for storage and retrieval, and create dashboards to track performance data.
- Find ways to standardise activities: design your own templates to collect data from others, use online survey creation tools, create flowcharts and infographics and make training videos for standard processes.

10

SET BOUNDARIES

Why we need boundaries

We only have a set amount of time each day, but the demands on us outstrip the finite resource. So to be truly productive, it makes sense to limit those demands by setting boundaries. The main elements involved in meeting demands are:

- How much work we accept;
- How long we spend doing it;
- The level of energy we apply to it;
- How much stress we allow it to cause.

I found a metaphor for this in 'Boost Your Productivity and Achieve Your Goals' by Matt Avery (link). He talked about a goldfish bowl, but I've never seen one of those with an outlet tap, so I've created my own version.

Let's imagine a drinks dispenser. I thought this might have more appeal; feel free to choose your own tipple! It has an opening at the top to pour in the drink (the work we're asked to do) and a tap at the bottom to let out the drink (completed tasks).

We can't change the dispenser's size; it can only take so much work, and if we overload it, it will start to overflow. All that wine (oops, water) is a messy pool on the floor, as we will be if we keep trying to do the impossible. We can't change the flow from the tap either; we can only complete a certain amount in the time available.

The only thing we can change is the top, where work comes in. We can make small changes to how we do the tasks inside the dispenser, but it's the volume that causes pressure and panic. By now, I hope I've convinced you that overloading yourself damages your productivity, sapping your energy and reducing the quality of your work.

You are not being lazy if you try to limit the amount you accept. You're being pragmatic, wanting to perform the important tasks well.

This is why we need boundaries. Read on to learn how to set them.

Saying yes or no

Being honest and saying no to a non-essential request which is outside your remit when you have no capacity for it is fundamental to controlling the flow of work into your dispenser.

Do you end up saying yes because it's too hard to say no? Do you always agree to extra demands from anyone, even if you're working flat out to meet an impossible deadline? Why do you think this is? Can you describe the sensation you get when someone asks you to do something unexpected which you don't want to do?

Saying yes unwillingly can be uncomfortable. You might worry that the person who asked will think you're rejecting them, rather than the request. You may believe you'll be regarded as unhelpful or uncaring. A more common reaction is guilt for letting the person down. How we love to pile guilt on ourselves!

If this sounds like you, please try to stop this habit; you are not obliged to please everyone. If you depend on other people's approval, it suggests their opinion of you matters more than your own opinion of yourself.

This all means you take the path of least conflict and give in to the other person, putting their needs ahead of your own. It will make you less effective in the things which matter to you. It won't even occur to them that you don't want to/can't do it; they'll just be relieved at passing it on. They will go away happy and will inevitably return and try it on again. You, on the other hand, will probably feel resentful the whole time you're doing the task, and end up in a negative spiral.

It's important to listen to your inner voice when it tells you you're uncomfortable with a request, or if you really don't have room in your schedule for it. If you say yes without thinking, you might be stuck with a task you either dread or can't do unless you demote something else on your list.

It can happen in our personal life too; family or friends often assume we will do something because we've never said no before. It can be even harder to be assertive with people you know and love.

Activity 18 - What could you have refused?

18.1 Look back over the last couple of months and make a list of the things outside your remit which you didn't want to do but ended up doing anyway.
18.2 Make some notes in your workbook about each situation: your feelings at the time, and how you could have handled it differently. Could you have said no to anything? What would have been the consequences, for them and for you?
18.3 If you think refusal would have damaged your relationship with the person, are you sure? Does it hinge on their expectation that you'll drop everything and run to their assistance? Consider the boundaries and dynamics of the relationship. Most things can be handled with understanding on both sides.

How to say no comfortably
You can learn to avoid the discomfort of saying no by taking

control of the conversation. Be aware of someone trying to manipulate you by making you feel guilty for refusing.

Your responsible position gives you the right to organise your time to give maximum attention to your most important work. You'll be saying yes to many genuine requests, so a few 'No' responses are acceptable in cases which are neither important nor urgent, especially when the requester is perfectly capable of doing them!

To stay purposeful and productive, weigh up every request before answering, and say no to non-essential tasks which would have a negative impact on your ability to stay on top of things. It's harder if someone has a genuine reason for asking, but if it would cause you extra stress, you are entitled to protect your own well-being.

In saying you should weigh up a request, I don't mean that in every case you should delay a decision by saying you'll get back to the person. They'll go away believing there's a chance you'll say yes, and you'll be left plucking up the courage to contact them with a refusal, which is much harder than saying no on the spot.

Think quickly, trust your instinct, and then give a firm decision. Some decisions are harder, so you might say 'I'm sorry, I can't right now, but if I'm in a position to do it some other time, I'll let you know'. If it's not urgent, it's better to say no first and then work out a way of helping later, rather than agree to do it but let them down.

When a more senior colleague is making the request, it's obviously harder to say no, but you can put the question back to them in a way that makes them realise it would cause overload. Ask them whether it's more important than task x, y and z. Ask them to choose which task you can drop or delay in order to do the new one. It's possible they genuinely don't appreciate how heavy your workload is.

A tactic which can help you say no on the spot is to imagine some scenarios and create a few responses in advance. It's easier to remember one you've prepared earlier than to invent one quickly. It also avoids you being drawn into lying out of desperation, then getting caught out doing something else!

Here's a revelation: you don't have to give a reason. Oprah Winfrey once said 'No is a complete sentence'. You can simply say

'I'm sorry, I can't.' They may be so taken aback that they forget to ask why!

However, psychology experiments suggest giving a reason is more likely to make people give way. It appeals to the rational part of the brain, regardless of how strong or weak the reason is! Don't feel obliged to go into details; you might give them an opening to persuade you. Be firm and give a clear and simple reason.

Your pre-prepared responses could be something like 'I'm sorry, I can't, because I have an urgent piece of work to do', 'because it isn't a good fit for my skills', or 'because I'm already fully committed.'

If you get a bad reaction, don't be drawn into discussing it and don't change your mind. If you do, they'll continue to manipulate you, now they know which buttons to press!

I've been consciously re-balancing my work since my husband retired, and I've said no to several consultancy assignments, either because they would be too intensive, require a longer-term input, or because I have other commitments. As a freelancer, I realise I have complete freedom, but my point is that everyone has understood, and it was a relief to say no rather than fail to do my best work.

Try to develop the art of saying no when you can do it reasonably. You have nothing to lose and much to gain.

Activity 19 - Your 'saying no' phrases

19.1 Use your examples from the last activity to construct some 'No' phrases to use in similar situations in the future.
19.2 Visualise yourself saying them to someone you know.
Practise, so you can speak confidently if an occasion arises.

Know enough

Knowledge is crucial to performing well in a fast-changing profession like education. If, like me, you love learning for its own sake, this could be another area where you need to set boundaries.

Do you need to read every policy paper or announcement produced by the government? Don't fall into the trap of thinking you need to fully understand all the educational aspects of the school. There is a threshold beyond which it won't add value.

If you need to know something specific, such as how decisions on staff deployment are arrived at for Integrated Curriculum Led Financial Planning, arrange a session with the member of staff who does the timetable. You don't need to understand all the intricacies; you just need answers to straightforward questions from the wizard. Yes, I regard timetabling as a dark art; us Muggles have no chance of understanding it. So don't try. Stick to what you need to know for your current role, and the next post if you're actively looking.

You obviously need to be on top of funding and finance issues and any others which change frequently. I've already mentioned my School Financial Success (SFS) monthly newsletter, which is completely free. It contains a list of government finance and funding announcements from the previous month, with links so you can click on those most relevant to you. You can sign up via the red button on my home page: https://schoolfinancialsuccess.com.

For wider education policy updates, there are document summary services, such as those provided by The School Bus (link) and Bristol University (link). The Key (link) also provides online access to a wide range of articles and guidance. There are free services but even paid ones can be excellent value when you consider your time saving. Some LAs subscribe to these services and make them available to schools, in which case you only need to find the right person to add you to the distribution list.

Think more widely about ways to enhance your knowledge besides the obvious books, courses, coaching and mentoring. Look for signposts to summary information as a shortcut. You can explore podcasts,

YouTube videos, LinkedIn, Facebook and Twitter. Follow the right people for access to the latest headlines and analysis, and use their links to find the source documents if needed.

Delay, delegate or eliminate

This section discusses the tactics to apply to quadrant 2, 3 and 4 tasks. They help to limit the flow of work into the dispenser by delaying tasks, delegating them or getting rid of them completely.

This isn't a one-off exercise; you need to be vigilant and watch for the volume creeping up again. When planning your week, do a quick check to see if you really are the only person who can do the work.

Delay

Delaying is suited to quadrant 2, the less urgent but still important tasks which you can't delegate. It isn't always possible if you have external timescales for statutory returns, budgeting, and closure of accounts, to name a few. But you will have some freedom over the timing of items such as projects, reviews of policies and processes, income generation and preparing for expiry of contracts.

A good starting point is to identify items whose timing you can control, as an initial list of candidates for delaying. What would be the impact if you did them later? Would it adversely affect your finances, or the availability of staff to help?

Check that the timescales for actions in your business plan are realistic, given the other things likely to occur at the same time. You'll need to revise them if something unexpected crops up. For example, if you have to construct a deficit recovery plan urgently to get approval for your budget, you may need the agreement of your Chair of Governors or Trustees to reschedule some policy reviews. If you have an extension clause in a contract, you can trigger it to delay a re-tendering exercise, as long as the provider is performing well.

In some cases, bringing a project forward might be better than a delay. For example, if a project is scheduled to start just as you're preparing next year's budget and closing the accounts, you could start the information gathering and planning stage earlier. This has an added benefit: your subconscious will be beavering away on it, producing ideas and solutions ready for when you pick it up again.

Delegate

There's a tendency in public services to promote people into management posts because they excel at their job, but managing staff is very different from a technical role. It's easy to fall into the trap of protecting valued staff, instead of practising delegation.

Which tasks are best suited to you? Are they a good use of your time? If you are the only person with the skills and qualifications for a significant project and it will enhance your profile and help to realise your goals, it's probably an easy decision. In the long run, it's best to train others in less critical tasks and free up your time for strategic work.

As a self-confessed control freak, I know it's hard to let go. But we need to develop others, to build capacity, allow them fulfilment, retain staff, and achieve succession planning. The key is to define the task well and ensure staff have the knowledge and skills to do it. As long as you have monitoring systems, you'll be able to keep an eye on progress with minimal risk.

Always build in a buffer when giving someone a deadline; you won't achieve your own timescales if others don't deliver their part in time. But make sure you check the information as soon as it comes in, otherwise your cover will be blown! Your colleagues won't appreciate it if they provide a report to you by the deadline you've set, then a week later they receive an email from you saying it needs more attention.

Eliminate

Over time, if you absorb additional work and keep doing it without ever testing if it's essential or not, you encourage an expectation that you will take on more responsibilities. You might also continue doing unnecessary work long after it's become redundant.

Create a common set of questions you can use to decide whether a task or a process is necessary or not. Then you'll only need to add a few specific questions when a situation arises.

You won't always be able to eliminate a whole task. If you suspect part of an existing process is no longer needed, try asking those who carry it out; they know most about it. I bet they can identify pointless parts of a system, or something which isn't working as well as it should. Just be cautious; some staff may have a vested interest in keeping their part of a process intact, and won't 'fess up.

If you do identify things which you can stop, delay or reduce, keep an eye out for any detrimental impact on another team or person in the school, and make sure you're still complying with funding body requirements. A collective approach will prevent problems and encourage staff to come up with ideas to reduce burdens.

Activity 20 - Delay, delegate, eliminate

20.1 Consider your routine tasks and processes. Identify a series of questions to expose potential eliminations or adjustments and list them in your workbook, where you'll find some prompts.
20.2 Use the advice in this chapter to add appropriate actions to your planning document for the items on your list.
20.3 Look at all the quadrant 2, 3 and 4 actions in your planning document and check you have the right actions and timescales for delaying, delegating and eliminating as required.

Manage expectations

You may find your relationships with other staff in the school play a part in setting effective boundaries. At the heart of this are your expectations of each other. It's a two-way street; you need to understand what people expect of you and what you expect from others.

What others expect of you

Having a clear job description (JD) and knowing what your manager expects of you will bring a clearer focus to your role. I've used 'manager' as a generic term whatever the hierarchy. Education moves so fast that JDs can quickly become out of date; everyone is so busy responding to new policies that the allocation of duties can change by stealth.

Be sure the expectations placed upon you are realistic. They need to recognise the extent of your responsibilities, the support available, where you sit in the school's structure, and your salary level. Support could come from in-house staff, central teams in an academy trust, local authority service level agreements, school partnerships, contracts or consultancy. The situation will vary according to your size and phase of school.

Talking to other SBPs might help you to identify whether you are overloaded compared to those with similar roles in your phase and size of school. Use SBP networks in the DfE's list (link), or if you don't have one locally, why not reach out to others and start one?

When making comparisons, bear in mind that others may have a different leadership structure and could organise support functions in varying ways, especially if they are part of a Multi-Academy Trust. These differences could affect how responsibilities are shared out.

If you are struggling, try to self-assess your workload. One way of doing this is to do a time tracking exercise, which you did at the beginning of this book (Activity 2) and which you'll be analysing in the next chapter as a time management tool. You can also review the contents of your planners. They will show your workload over a longer timescale than the time tracker sample, highlighting when the pressures are particularly acute.

This can all produce evidence about the tensions you're facing from the volume, complexity and timeliness of your tasks, and show up conflicting priorities and impossible deadlines. It will also highlight the demands being placed on you by other staff across the school. It's all valuable information to lend weight to your argument for a more reasonable workload.

What to do with the information

Your next steps will depend on your findings. You may simply need to tweak your systems to become more efficient. But if you genuinely believe the expectations on you are unrealistic, you need to talk to your manager about it. Don't struggle on and suffer increasing stress without at least trying to broach the subject. Too many SBPs are reluctant to admit to their manager that they are overwhelmed, as if it's an admission of defeat. But it's far better to raise the subject and have a rational discussion than let it affect your physical and/or mental health.

Don't assume the overload is deliberate. Your manager might not appreciate what it actually takes to do the role; it's easy to underestimate what someone else does. This is the trouble when you make it appear easy!

Opening up the conversation might be daunting, but if you don't, you can't reasonably expect things to improve, can you? Marshal your facts and approach it in a professional manner. Start with the positives: explain how much you're achieving, then highlight the difficulties you're experiencing and show how they're limiting your effectiveness.

Take your evidence with you, to provide a focus for the meeting and make it easier to explain the specific issues which are causing the difficulties. A vague speech about how you're struggling can be more easily dismissed or given less weight than it deserves. If you are seen to be well prepared, it's much harder for your manager to resist a proper discussion.

Your likelihood of success will increase if you can suggest some potential solutions. I was ever so grateful to staff who did this, and more inclined to react favourably! The big benefit for you is being able to put forward ideas which are in your interest. You'll have had time to think them through, and you'll be better prepared.

Solutions could involve shuffling responsibilities, training someone else, getting temporary expertise in from an external source or from within the MAT for an academy, re-prioritising projects or tasks, helping your manager see a task isn't essential, or changing the frequency and deadlines for management reporting. Part of the trouble with being an SBP is you are ultra cautious about spending money, but you can get creative and find alternative ways of easing the load.

This will turn the meeting into a problem-solving session rather than a whinge-fest, and you'll stand more chance of success than if you expect your manager to identify options.

Your expectations of others

If you're a manager, you also need to be crystal clear about your expectations of team members. Does everyone have a clear job description, reviewed regularly to pick up changes in systems or processes? Does everyone understand the boundaries between roles within the team, to avoid duplication of effort and gaps? Is your performance management system working effectively?

Don't let others 'put the monkey on your back', i.e. move tasks to you which they should be doing. If the issue is a lack of ability or confidence, provide the training they need. Moral support could be needed if they're struggling; monitor their performance for a while until their confidence grows. Do some probing to find out why they don't feel able to do it; try to make them see what's possible.

Sometimes people downplay their abilities because they have discovered it's a way of avoiding additional duties. Or they may actively be looking for someone who they can pass work to, for an easier life. This can often happen with people outside of your team; they know you are always willing to help and somehow they manage to transfer a job to you, often using flattery to get you to agree to it. This isn't cynicism, honestly… it's experience!

Do you have a Last Minute Lottie or Larry in your school? Have a response ready and train them to be better organised. If you value your job, your wording obviously needs to be tailored to the person. I like 'Lack of planning on your part does not constitute an emergency on mine'! But for others you'll have to bite your tongue and say 'I'm sorry, I already have a tight deadline on a top priority task.' This reminds them you have other commitments and a system to identify what's important.

Can you think of a Manipulative Maurice or Moana? Can you identify what's going on? Why did they try to take advantage of you by passing work across, and more to the point, how did they succeed? What can you do next time to avoid it happening again?

There's lots of advice on staff management for you to explore. One of my beta readers recommends 'Successful Difficult Conversations in School' by Sonia Gill (link).

Activity 21 - Managing expectations

21.1 Use all available sources to make an honest assessment of whether the demands on you are reasonable or not.

21.2 Do some free writing about how you can tackle the situation, and act on it, e.g. gathering evidence to discuss with your manager, or finding ways to increase your efficiency.

21.3 Make notes on how you convey your expectations to staff. Think up some ideas using the advice in this chapter.

21.4 Where appropriate, build actions into your planning document.

Key points

- Set boundaries in order to limit the demands on you. Think of your situation like a drinks dispenser; you can't change its size, or the outlet tap, so all you can control is the amount of work going into it.
- Don't let others pass on non-essential and non-urgent tasks which are outside your remit if they are capable of doing them, or if it would cause you pressure.
- Learn how to say no instead of yes without feeling guilty.
- Only learn what you need to know for your current role and the next steps. Find shortcuts to keep informed, including subscribing to newsletters and following key people on social media.
- Make a plan to tackle the items with delay, delegate and eliminate flags in your planning document. Watch for interdependencies and understand the impact of your proposed actions.
- Managing expectations will smooth relationships and help you set boundaries. Aim for clarity in what others expect of you, and what you expect of them. If you are overloaded, gather evidence and suggest potential solutions to your manager.

11

TIME MANAGEMENT

Achieve more

We all have the same number of hours in a day, and some people achieve more than others with them. But what others do isn't important; what matters is what you do with your hours, in your context and with your talents. Time is money, so try to squeeze every drop of value from the opportunities open to you. Don't worry about what anyone else is doing.

In this chapter, I will encourage you to take a helicopter view of your time management and I'll offer some suggestions about how to tackle common areas of difficulty and sharpen up your practice.

Track your time

In Activity 2, I asked you to track how you spent your time before reading the rest of this book. Now we'll be analysing the results.

Your time, focus and attention are key to making things happen, but they are all in limited supply. It's important to decide how to spend them, if you want to become more efficient. Before you completed the tracker, would you have been confident about how much time you spent on concentrated work, interruptions from others or periods spent checking social media? Are you flitting from one thing to another and not finishing any of them in a timely manner?

Once you understand your baseline and know what you need to improve, you can repeat the time tracking exercise at intervals for a reality check. But use it as a positive tool, not a stick to beat yourself with. No one is expected to work at top speed every single hour of every day, so don't give yourself a hard time over the results.

This tool helps you compare what you've actually been doing with what you think you've been doing. It will reveal whether you're paying attention to the important parts of your role or putting everyone else first. Once you have this information, you can unpick what's going on. What's stopping you from getting the essentials done? Are you wasting time on trivial matters? Are there things on your To Do list which you need to let go of? They may have been important a while ago, but circumstances might have changed.

Analysing the results

I asked you to do the tracker at the start so you could get some distance from it while reading up to this point. Now you can return to it to analyse the results. You're looking for patterns. Did you manage to create some quality uninterrupted blocks, or does it show lots of distractions as you flit between tiny tasks? This will indicate the extent of your attention-switching; I'll explain this more in the next chapter, but for now I'll just say it's the worst thing you can do.

Do the interruptions happen at particular times of day, and do they involve particular individuals? How long do they last? How have they affected your ability to meet deadlines, complete a task to a satisfactory standard, or offer your support to other staff?

Are you taking enough breaks? Do you get some exercise each day? Are you regularly getting a good amount of sleep (whatever you need), and is it unbroken?

Once you've identified the unhelpful patterns, you're in a position to do something about them, using the various chapters in this book to choose your bespoke solutions. As you take specific actions to improve your productivity, you can repeat your time tracking. You'll be able to compare your new pattern with the baseline and see if the changes have had a positive impact.

I found this was an excellent tool for reviewing my routines. It showed plenty of sustained blocks of intensive work, but I tended to prolong my breaks by following threads on social media and reading interesting articles. I now leave my phone and iPad in another room when I have a tight deadline to meet.

You might prefer a different approach for analysing your working patterns and distractions, and that's perfectly fine. Just make sure you can detect the areas that need attention.

Activity *22 - Time tracking reflections*

22.1 Return to your initial time tracker and analyse the results to detect any patterns. Ask yourself some questions along the lines I've suggested above, to identify your main areas of inefficiency.

22.2 How could you spend your day more productively? Do some free writing about what you need to change and how to approach it.

22.3 Turn these into actions and schedule them or put reminders in an appropriate place for behavioural changes.

The main purpose of this activity is to identify what's interrupting your flow and decide what you need to work on. It should help you stick to your own agenda instead of following someone else's, and limit the distractions. This is a nice transition to our next section, which is all about interruptions, the bane of our lives!

Minimise interruptions

Now I imagine we're getting to the crux of your problems. It certainly used to be mine, when I was working in busy open plan offices. Handling interruptions is such a vital part of managing your time. They disturb your flow and make you lose track of where you were.

Minimising interruptions is a mindset issue. It's about valuing yourself and seeing time as a commodity; you only have so much, and it needs to be spent well. Don't give away your best to others; guard it with your life and keep it for your most important duties.

This can be tricky to get right; it requires a balanced approach. You might have an 'Open Door' policy, but I hope this doesn't mean you have to be available every minute of the day, ready to drop a vital, urgent task to deal with someone's tiny irritation or provide information they can reasonably be expected to know or look up for themselves. I bet you're already thinking about the usual suspects!

This is about mutual respect and support, allowing everyone to do their important work while setting a reasonable amount of time for helping others. Could you broker an agreement among the staff in your office to agree not to interrupt each other during set periods, unless it's about a genuinely urgent and essential issue? It's all too easy to be drawn into a discussion when you're in close proximity.

Asking everyone to save up queries then run through them with the relevant colleague at a designated time is a much better use of valuable capacity. If you know there's a list, you'll be more likely to be business-like in tackling it, with less chat than if it began with a casual wander up to someone else's desk. I'm not against socialising, but there's a time and place for it, and it's not when you're rushing against the clock to submit an important return.

Clearly it's harder to deal with interruptions from more senior colleagues. One would hope they are less likely to do it for insignificant matters, but if not, would a more regular catch-up slot help?

For interruptions from everyone else in the school, some forward planning might help. If your calendar is visible to everyone, can you diary meetings with yourself to complete important tasks? Teachers are allowed 10% planning and preparation time, so why should you feel guilty for taking the same approach? People are (hopefully) less likely to interrupt if they think you're in a meeting. For added benefit, find a different room. If this isn't possible, you can arrange for a trusted member of staff to take messages, then put a 'Do Not Disturb' sign on your door or desk, asking people to go to them instead.

If someone comes in saying 'Are you busy?' when you're in the middle of a crucial task, do you shrug or say nothing, giving them unspoken consent to interrupt?

Why not practice a different response, as we considered in the section on saying No? Try something like: 'Actually I'm just at a critical point. Is it ok if I come and find you at (insert a time)?'. Most reasonable people will agree. If they insist it will only take a minute, say 'I'm sorry, it really isn't a good time for me, unless it's genuinely urgent.' If they confirm it is super-urgent, ask them to sum up the issue in one sentence, so you can decide how to respond.

Interruptions might be initiated by other people, but you don't have to accept them, especially phone calls. Receptionists should be good gatekeepers, able to relay a message instead of putting the call through. If it's a direct call and you recognise the number, let them leave a message. A number you don't recognise is likely to be a scam or sales call. In a genuinely urgent case, the caller will find a way to get to you. Having a designated slot for responding to answerphone messages will make you speed through them.

When a piece of work is time critical, do you put your phone on silent and switch off notifications? Or do you jump like one of Pavlov's dogs and pick it up whenever it pings?

There's an app called Forest (link) which can stop you from touching your phone. When you want to stay focused, you plant a virtual tree in the app. While you do your work, the tree grows, but leaving the app part way through your task will make the tree die. Its unique feature is the ability to earn virtual coins which you spend on real trees. The Forest team donates money to a partner organisation, 'Trees for the Future', and creates planting orders. It's another example of 'gamification', with visual stimulation and an incentive to stay productive, as well as allowing you to help the environment.

Working from home

If you find you can't reduce interruptions to a bearable level, consider asking for permission to work from home, either as a one-off or on a regular basis. Even one half-day per week can make a significant difference. You are far more likely to complete your tasks, and it will lift the weight of tight deadlines from your shoulders.

You can refer back to the section in chapter 3 on productivity in a crisis for tips on working from home. Tell colleagues in advance that you won't be available for calls except in a dire emergency. If they ignore this and ring for non-urgent reasons, be firm; ask them for a brief explanation so you can triage it. If it's not essential, tell them you'll call them back when it's convenient.

Letting someone interrupt encourages them to make it a habit. You can scan emails and decide not to respond, so why not take the same approach to phone calls? If you do choose to answer, don't let the caller waffle on or engage in chit-chat.

Make sure you have the concentrated blocks of time needed to finish the task. If you're at home and your internet goes down, will you be able to access the files you need? Anticipate it and make them available offline or download them. Otherwise you'll need to contact the office to get them sent, creating a perfect opportunity for them to ask you a question or tell you something which you'll then worry about!

Self-inflicted interruptions

Some interruptions are down to our own lack of self-discipline. I'm guilty of dipping into email when I lose my focus. I read an email with a link and open it, then realise I shouldn't be looking at it. So I stop, but leave the tab open, intending to return to it later. When I go to my browser to look something up, I'm distracted by the page still being there, and I start reading.

This is attention-switching at its finest; the pages remain in my head and the awareness of them can easily disrupt my thought flow. It's far more productive to do ninety minutes of focused work on a report or piece of financial analysis than to spend three hours jumping around from one task to another. Trust me: I've done both frequently!

Social media is probably responsible for more self-inflicted interruptions than anything else. The first question to ask is why you are using each platform. Does scrolling through Facebook, Twitter, Instagram and Pinterest directly contribute to your best work and meet your deadlines? I suspect most of it doesn't, apart from specific questions and support in SBL communities. Go to your profiles and note the frequency and timing of your posts. What should you have been doing then? Yes, tough love again!

Ask yourself whether each social media account is helping you achieve your goals. Do the positives outweigh the negatives? Reduce the number of apps you use and you'll cut the potential distractions. Be disciplined and only use them in low-energy periods, when you've completed your important tasks.

Self-inflicted interruptions are often prompted by discomfort of some kind, such as boredom or tiredness. We'll talk more about this when we explore resistance and procrastination later.

Removing the source is one tactic, but that isn't always practical if you need to look up some information. Another approach is to schedule tasks in blocks of time in a way that creates variety, without switching tasks too often.

Sometimes you can be tempted into browsing other websites while searching for something. Planning ahead will help with this. Before embarking on a complex task, check you have everything to hand, so you don't need to break off and lose your train of thought.

If all else fails, an app like Rescuetime (link) might help. You select which sites to classify as time wasting, and it sorts your usage into different categories with a productivity score for the day. Focusbooster (link) is similar, allowing you to track how you're spending your time.

Activity 23 - Tackling interruptions

23.1 Using the evidence from your tracker and your own instincts, list in your workbook the most common and significant interruptions you face.
23.2 Refer to the tips in this section and identify the actions you plan to take to limit these interruptions.

Master your email

Is your inbox bulging with out-of-date emails? A desk overflowing with paper is obvious, but a cluttered email system can also prey on your mind and affect your productivity. There are two main issues: reducing a backlog and keeping on top of ongoing emails.

Tackling a backlog

Try sorting emails by person rather than by date. Some people copy others in routinely when it's unnecessary; you can quickly spot these and do some bulk deleting. If you can see a thread of emails, you can delete all the earlier versions, rather than filing duplicates. Alternatively, change your settings to group emails by conversation.

Set aside a daily slot when your energy is lower and tackle the backlog gradually. Create a sensible folder structure.

Managing ongoing email traffic

To stay on top of emails, there are two important rules: designate specific slots for email activity rather than constantly dipping in and out, and aim to handle each email as few times as possible.

I usually check my emails three times a day including one major session for action/responses, depending on my priorities for the day. If I keep looking at them, it becomes a huge time waster and a distraction. I'm also likely to break rule number two by re-opening some to check the contents rather than dealing with them.

Here's a potential system for dealing with your inbox:

- Do an initial scan of emails received yesterday.
- Move any needing attention into an Action folder, to be dealt with today. Flag the vital ones.
- Resolve that any more arriving today will be dealt with tomorrow, unless they are urgent and important.
- Deal with the rest as quickly as possible: detach and save essential attachments, forward those which other people need to act on, file emails only if essential, and delete others. Your Inbox should contain only one day's emails.
- Tackle the Action folder in your dedicated session, flagged emails first. Handle all emails decisively.

Whatever your approach, get emails out of the way as quickly as you can, so the difficult or contentious ones don't hang around, preying on your mind and disrupting your flow. You can pursue the important things and be confident that you have a system to capture high priority emails and deal with them at an appropriate point.

Review your use of email

Take a look through your email exchanges, both sent and received. Are they full of chit-chat, or clear and purposeful? Do you ask open questions which make recipients uncertain about how to respond, or direct, closed questions demanding a specific answer?

Are multiple people copied in for information unnecessarily? Can they get the details in a regular briefing or newsletter? Is there a trail of responses bouncing around, so you can't tell who's answered?

Make sure your emails contain clear steps to be followed by the recipient. If you avoid confusion, they won't have any excuse to waffle. Keep emails business-like and limit the use of the Copy field to the essential people. Don't respond if an email doesn't warrant it.

Turn off notifications. If you are always accessible and jump to answer emails as soon as they arrive, I guarantee you'll get more of them! Your colleagues will soon realise it is an easier way of getting information than looking it up for themselves.

Agree an email approach in your school

For real success, establish a common approach to email in your school, or at least in a smaller group. Every little helps. Meet up to share your main gripes about email, then identify some solutions.

For example, you could agree to do any or all of the following:

- Speak in person if it's an urgent matter, to reduce the risk of someone not seeing the email early enough and avoid inboxes being clogged up with reminders.
- Resist copying in everyone for no particular reason.
- Tackle emails in batches and resist the temptation to keep checking your inbox. You know urgent requests will be made in person or by telephone.

Activity 24 - Mastering email

24.1 In your workbook, jot down your plans for tackling the backlog of emails and keeping on top of new ones from this point onwards.

24.2 Arrange an agenda item at your next team meeting to get ideas for a new approach to managing emails.

Time management tools

Throughout this book, you'll find examples of tools which will help you with specific productivity issues. I don't know every tool, so use your judgement and your innate curiosity to find others, but make sure they are suitable for your own circumstances.

In this section, I want to talk more generically about time management tools. I'll mention a few which don't appear elsewhere in the book, but they are by no means exhaustive.

Our brains can only hold so much information. Hands up anyone who's forgotten to do an urgent job. You can have a beautiful planner full of tasks, but if you don't look at it, you can be caught out. So you need to find tools to cover all your bases.

The aim of any tool is to simplify your life, help you focus on what's important, and shorten the time spent on routine tasks. So avoid the 'shiny new object' syndrome, because having too many can be counterproductive. Only look for a new tool when you have a well-defined problem which your existing tools or techniques can't solve.

You may be restricted by your school's systems, but it's worth discussing new tools. If there are no compatibility or security issues, you may be able to introduce them and help others. Think about what you use at home, too.

When you have identified a problem, ask yourself:

- What do I want to achieve?
- Do I already have the tools to help?
- If not, which new tools might solve my problem?
- How much time and effort does it take to learn them?
- Are they quick and easy to operate?
- How can I measure the results?

Asking colleagues and friends for recommendations is useful, but make sure they suit your own context and preferred way of working before you jump in. Others who have tried them will be able to give you clues about the main benefits and drawbacks, which you can then double check. You can take free trials, but don't flit between too many, or you'll waste precious time and confuse yourself!

Here are a few extra ideas for tools. They may be worth checking out if your own set up doesn't provide what you need.

Passwords

I did a double take when I saw a 'Passwords' notebook in a stationery shop a while ago. I can understand the temptation, when we're supposed to create unique passwords for everything; it's impossible to remember them all. But a physical record isn't a secure method; it can easily be lost and if it's stolen, you'll justifiably panic.

Enter 'Last Pass' (link), a free app which provides an online vault to store all your passwords. When activated on a device, it populates your ID and password fields for sites you've saved in the vault.

Only having to remember a single master password (never to be repeated anywhere else, obviously) to activate it is a real advantage. You can make your passwords as complicated as you like, without fear of forgetting them. The moments you save compared to typing in a password, forgetting and trying again all mount up too!

Managing meetings

You will probably have a meeting scheduler at school, but if not, or if you have to organise meetings in a personal capacity, Doodle polls make it a doddle (sorry, I couldn't resist!). Doodle (link) can be synchronised with Google Cal, Office 365 or iCal. Once options are set for dates and times, a link is emailed to everyone and it reports back on their availability. It beats the multitude of back-and-forth emails you get when scheduling a meeting manually.

Creating documents

Occasionally you need to create documents with images or info-graphics to draw attention to an important point. Visuals can be effective but time-consuming to create. I've already mentioned Canva.com which provides a range of templates for infographics, newsletters, calendars, posters, flyers, brochures, and presentations. You can prefix any of the menu items with 'education' in the search to find the most relevant ones. The Canva Pro Version is free for schools; it's a great time saver and so simple, you can give it to someone else to do!

Key points

- What matters is how you make your time count, in your context and with your talents.
- Track your time to see the balance between your focused work and interruptions, and identify where you can make changes. Set a baseline against which you can measure your progress.
- Develop a different mindset for handling interruptions and claim back more time for your important tasks. Know how to deal with those initiated by other people and recognise the self-inflicted ones.
- Review your approach to managing emails, tackle the backlog and start a new system for keeping your inbox clear. Spread the good practice to others in your school for maximum impact.
- Choose your time management tools wisely. Avoid too many and make sure they are fit for purpose and suited to your context.

PART IV

MAXIMISE

Maximise

Organise

Set the foundations

You're making great progress, with a plan in place to focus on your most important tasks.

Now let's learn some superpowers to help you soar in the productivity stakes. In this part, we'll be covering ways to achieve a flow state for focused work, tackle resistance, build capacity, and hone your skills.

It's time to invest in yourself and reap the rewards, so fasten your seat belts!

12

ACHIEVE FLOW

What 'flow' means

It's all very well minimising interruptions and improving your time management skills, but if you can't focus on the important work you need to do, then it will all have been in vain.

The key to completing complex tasks is getting into a 'flow state', where you can easily summon up full concentration with a minimum of effort. This can be difficult if you are in a busy environment such as an open plan office, but it's not impossible.

Mihaly Csikszentmihalyi, an expert in positive psychology, was the first to identify and study flow. He identified eight features:

1. Complete concentration on the task;
2. Clarity of goals, keeping the reward in mind, and immediate feedback;
3. Transformation of time (speeding up/slowing down);
4. The experience is intrinsically rewarding;
5. Effortlessness and ease;
6. A good balance between perceived challenge and perceived skills;

7. Actions and awareness are merged, removing self-conscious rumination;
8. A feeling of control over the task.

Flow happens when you are in the right place mentally and physically to focus on a specific task. The barriers to it are constant distractions and interruptions. Habits like leaving multiple windows open in your browser or allowing pop-up notifications act as friction, preventing you moving smoothly through your tasks.

Do you let distractions take over your day? Imagine a typical morning. Your computer pings as an email arrives, grabbing your attention. It won't take long, you think, as you set aside what you were doing and start to reply. The phone rings, another message arrives, or someone walks into the office wanting information which they could look up themselves. You try to return to the report you should be writing, and you struggle to remember where you were up to.

Soon the morning has passed, and you still haven't ticked anything off your list. Anxiety sets in; the deadline's looming, and you'll have to do it tonight, when you're tired and you know it will take you twice as long. Deluged with information, you're losing the ability to identify what's important. The more you worry about something, the more negative you feel about it, and the more you'll resist, which gives you a stronger conviction that it's impossible.

It doesn't have to be this way; you can find ways to remove the friction which is stopping you getting into a flow state. But first let's explore what's going on when you frequently switch between tasks.

Deep work principles

One of my favourite books on productivity is 'Deep Work' by Cal Newport, subtitled 'Rules for focused success in a distracted world' (link). It transformed my ability to get things done by showing me how to build a habit of concentrating on one task at a time. There are lots of fascinating concepts in this book. In this section, I will explain the ideas which are most relevant to achieving a flow state.

Newport's definition of deep work is:

'Professional activities performed in a state of distraction-free concentration that push your cognitive capabilities to their limit. These efforts create new value, improve your skill, and are hard to replicate.'

Deep work needs a sustained period of uninterrupted thinking. Many prolific people hide themselves away; in the SBP world this is not exactly easy to do for long periods, but is achievable in shorter bursts. Deep work is essential for learning. With such rapid changes in education, especially in funding and technology, we need to grasp new things quickly and understand how to apply them.

The availability of network tools – email, messaging, social media and information sites – has fragmented our attention and trained us to need distractions. We're far more likely to be engaged in shallow work, which is less satisfying once the dopamine hit from a social media 'Like' or a reply evaporates, and it's also damaging, because it reduces our capacity for deep work.

So we need to create the right conditions for a flow state to get the important things done with less effort.

Avoiding multi-tasking

Multi-tasking can be regarded as a skill, but it's terrible for productivity. You can physically do more than one thing at a time; we can all walk and hold a conversation with someone else. But your brain can only actively pay attention to one thing. If I try to answer emails while listening to an instructional podcast, I only absorb part of what I'm hearing. In reality, multi-tasking is attention-switching.

If you're sceptical about this, there's a useful online test (link) which will hopefully convince you.

The problem is that the brain takes time to change tack. Newport quotes Sophie Leroy from the University of Minnesota, who identified an effect called 'attention residue'. When you switch tasks, your attention doesn't completely follow; a residue remains. Part of your brain is still stuck on the original (probably half-finished) task.

It might seem harmless to sneak a peek at your emails now and again, but as Leroy says, '*That quick check introduces a new target for your attention. Even worse, by seeing messages that you cannot deal with at the moment (which is almost always the case), you'll be forced to turn back to the primary task with a secondary task left unfinished. The attention residue left by such unresolved switches dampens your performance.*'

Some experts say it can take up to 17 minutes for the brain to get back into a task. If you switch your attention frequently, imagine how much time you're wasting in total, and how much more you'll get done if you can learn to focus for longer.

The theory of deep work

A central idea for achieving deep work is batching important tasks into long, uninterrupted stretches. By maximising the intensity, you get more done. This is how you can free up time for thinking and relaxation. Don't waste your deep work; reserve it for important projects and tasks which will raise your performance and profile.

In the SBP role, the word 'long' should be considered a relative concept, given the number of interruptions you have to put up with! Try going deep for shorter periods; you will gradually build up your powers of concentration into longer stretches. Batch items into whatever time blocks you can create.

Separating out different activities is beneficial. Creative and analytical tasks use different parts of your brain (right and left respectively), so if you write the narrative sections of a report in one session, you'll achieve a consistent tone and finish sooner than if you keep breaking off to do pieces of financial analysis for your tables.

As ever, this is about balance. There's a time and place for shallow work. Know when focused concentration will achieve better results.

Plan your day

Planning what you are going to do each day is a great help in improving your productivity. Not only does it allow you to batch items, but it also reduces the number of decisions you have to take throughout the day.

Your brain gets enough stimuli in the course of a normal routine, so it's your job to simplify things. Barack Obama famously had a full set of matching suits, shirts, ties and shoes, so he didn't waste precious time deciding what to wear each morning. What better reason do you need to do some coordinated clothes shopping?

Your ability to control your day will partly depend on your role and the culture of your organisation. Many SBPs struggle to get their own work done, because they spend so much time doing everyone else's. I hope you now have some ideas for changing this.

Tough love challenge time again: how restricted are you, really? I'd be surprised if you weren't allowed to organise your own work. If you are operating to a completely inflexible schedule, you might want to discuss the situation with your manager. Most reasonable employers measure success by what you achieve, not when you do it.

Take a moment to reflect on the assumptions you've made about your schedule. Do you plan your day, or do you assume there's no point, because of all the interruptions you get? Are you letting others dictate your working rhythm? Do you ever think about <u>when</u> you do things? Or do you just pick up a task at random, and drop it when something more urgent, important or interesting comes along?

I've found a real benefit in matching up my tasks with my mood and environment. Getting into a flow state requires a certain type of energy, and trying to force it can be counterproductive.

Identify the best time of day for tasks

Be aware of your energy patterns. Are you freshest in the morning, or does it take a few hours and lots of caffeine for you to get going? Do you notice a slump in your concentration at a particular point in the day? Are you a night owl, suddenly waking up late at night and able to concentrate best when everyone else is asleep?

If you try to swim against the tide, doing difficult tasks when your concentration is low, you'll waste precious energy battling with your natural tendencies. It's far better to go with the flow instead.

The secret is to work with those rhythms, matching them to the types of tasks you have to do. Know when you are most likely to achieve peak performance as opposed to weak performance. You'll need to allow some flexibility, as your energy patterns may not always be reliable, but a broad awareness will help you plan your day.

There are four stages to this process:

1. Work out when your energy is high or low;
2. Identify which of your tasks planned for this week have the highest and lowest impact on your goals;
3. Identify which tasks require the most effort and concentration and which are more straightforward;
4. Match up blocks of high energy periods with high impact tasks which require a lot of effort and concentration. Continue down the levels until you reach low impact, low effort tasks, to be done when you are tired or distracted.

Energy spikes tend to last around 90 minutes, suggesting this is an optimal block of time for maintaining your concentration. But you can test this out and find your own balance.

I can hear you laughing at the thought of being able to do something for 90 minutes without interruptions. Well, why not book it in your diary and find somewhere else to go and do the work? Honestly, I bet 99.9% of the time, the people who want to talk to you can wait for up to 90 minutes. You're the one who's making an assumption that they can't wait. If you're constantly available, you create an expectation of an immediate answer; it doesn't mean they're entitled to one.

Psychologists say unhappiness at work often comes from a lack of control over what you do. Matching tasks with your energy levels allows you a sense of control and ensures you get them done more efficiently.

. . .

Thinking more broadly

As a school business professional, you have a multi-faceted role. Try to be clear about which hat you're supposed to be wearing at any given point in the day. If you have a series of letters or emails to write, or a set of instructions for different processes, do them all in one session while you're in the flow. Systems should allow them to be scheduled for sending at different times. Your 'voice' will be consistent, and you'll get satisfaction from ticking several items off your list.

Can you apply these planning principles to your personal life? Identify what gives you satisfaction and helps you to achieve your goals, then focus on those things, not on what other people want or expect you to do. Why not have that long-overdue conversation with your loved ones about how domestic chores and family duties are shared out? If you involve them, they will see you are serious about rebalancing things and should be supportive.

Set the conditions for flow

In an ideal world, you'd be able to imagine an iron-clad safe in the corner of the room where you put all your distractions in it (even people!) and firmly shut the door. Then you'd turn to your most essential task and stay in a bubble until it's done.

Oh really? In a busy school where everyone wants their bit of you, and they want it now? In a bid to tackle this thorny issue, I've already suggested booking time with yourself in a different location to get your most important thing done, so you can focus on it and avoid thinking about all the other things waiting for your attention.

But if you can't escape to a different space or work from home, which under normal circumstances obviously isn't an option for 100% of your time, there are other ways of removing distractions to get into a flow state. They tend to be about creating rituals, with cues to start your routine and build productive habits.

The techniques I'm going to suggest rely on you not being interrupted (the fundamental requirement of a flow state), so you need to make others aware of the periods when you need to be left alone. This is not an unreasonable request!

Creating a virtual bubble (a pre-Covid-19 heading!)

First, consider your environment. Open-plan offices might be good for sparking ideas and keeping communication lines open, but they can be bad news for individual productivity; there are far too many distractions. As an Assistant Director, I had my own office. When I worked at another LA in a big room with senior managers from different disciplines around me, it was interesting but harder to concentrate. If you can't change your location, try to create routines and rituals to counteract any distractions.

When I'm writing, I use an Apple app called 'Brain Wave: 35 Binaural Programmes' (link); there are others for Android devices and some subscription services such as Brain FM (link) which has a free trial. I put on headphones and choose a setting, such as Focused and Alert, Concentration, or Critical Thinking (there are lots more, even Hangover Relief!). It pulses, imitating the brainwaves for the chosen state. You can overlay it with music or natural sounds such as a waterfall, waves on a beach, a rainforest or thunderstorms.

Warning: Please be aware that this type of app should not be used by people with certain brain conditions or those prone to seizures. You **MUST** check before using it. This article (link) explains it further, but you must do your own research. **Disclaimer:** I can not be held responsible for any problems which arise from using the app.

Whenever I use it, I can immediately zone out everything else and focus on my task. It's said you shouldn't upload music with lyrics, otherwise your brain gets distracted. You may also end up singing along, which could be embarrassing! I like the thunderstorm sounds.

You can tell the other occupants of your office that when you have your headphones on, you are doing a focused piece of work and mustn't be disturbed unless it's essential. You may need to resist the temptation to keep them on all day, though.

I've already covered meditation, but in 'Deep Work', Cal Newport recommends a variation: productive meditation, done while you're engaged in something routine like walking, showering or driving. Instead of concentrating on emptiness, you focus on a professional problem and dismiss any thoughts which aren't related to it.

This improves your ability to think deeply, resist distraction and return repeatedly to a well-defined problem. Don't let your brain repeatedly loop round what you know; push it to the next step of being creative, and solutions will pop up.

Essentially, you need to create a regular practice as a reliable way of getting into the flow state. Try mixing it with images and inspirational sayings on your walls to create visual cues.

The Pomodoro technique

Another technique for creating a flow state, which can be used in conjunction with others, is consciously setting the length of time you are going to spend in detailed concentration.

The Pomodoro technique dates from the 1980s and is so named because its inventor Francesco Cirillo used a tomato-shaped kitchen timer, the Italian for tomato being pomodoro. His book explains the technique (link).

In this method, you set a timer for a period and give a task your full concentration. An optimal block is generally regarded as 25 minutes, followed by a five-minute break, but you can play around with different periods to see what suits you. Three 25-minute periods with a five-minute break after each of them equals 90 minutes, which we've already seen is believed to be an effective span of time.

After three Pomodoros, you can have a longer break of 20 minutes or so. But in a busy school office, I'm guessing any more than that will be pretty difficult. Even one or two Pomodoros must be worth trying.

You must resist doing anything else during this time. Move your phone out of temptation's way, close your browser except for any window you need to complete the task, and make sure no one can interrupt you. Put up a sign if you need to. If anything intrudes into your thoughts, jot it down then return to the task.

If you're still struggling with the temptation to do something else, steel yourself against acting on it. Don't ignore it; stay with the urge for a moment and notice the sensation. What makes you want to switch? Is it fear, boredom, inadequacy, or confusion? Analysing the urge can make it go away. Congratulate yourself for not giving in, then return to the task. It will be easier next time.

When the timer signals the 25 minutes is up, stop and take your five-minute break without any screen time. If you open your emails, you'll introduce a problem or another task into your brain. Try your hardest not to do anything work-related. You can use the first couple of minutes of subsequent sessions to review what you've done before.

General advice

When you're doing a focused task, remember the general points I've already made elsewhere: keep hydrated, take regular breaks, do occasional stretches or a walk, and eat healthy snacks.

If you've tried your best, but it's still hard to maintain your focus, think of the end goal. If this doesn't work either, try a different task. Sometimes giving your routine a shake up is enough.

Despite our best attempts, we might have no choice but to set aside one task to attend to another. If so, make sure you leave it at a sensible point. If you can, complete the new piece of work in one go and get back to the original one as soon as you can.

Do the worst thing first

There's nothing worse than having a dreaded task on your mind all day. You put it off, but it sits there, prodding at you, gradually getting bigger and bigger. The best way is to get it out of the way first, then you can forget about it and move on to something more palatable.

This strategy was given a charming name by Brian Tracy: Eat That Frog (link). On his website (link) he summarises it like this:

'*Mark Twain once said that if the first thing you do each morning is to eat a live frog, you can go through the day with the satisfaction of knowing that that is probably the worst thing that is going to happen to you all day long. Your "frog" is your biggest, most important task, the one you are most likely to procrastinate on if you don't do something about it.'*

When I eventually tackle the 'frog' I've been dreading, I often find it's not half as bad as I anticipated. I'll talk more about this soon.

Create downtime

Are you working solidly, taking minimal breaks, continuing after your day has finished, sometimes until late at night? I bet you don't feel refreshed when you wake, or if you do, it won't last long. By the afternoon, you'll struggle to focus on your planned tasks.

I make no apologies for returning to the theme of self-care, because it underpins your ability to get into a flow state. You need downtime, spaces during your waking hours when you can take a break. If you finish a task early, don't automatically fill the space with more work. Recharge your internal batteries in whatever way suits you.

But there's more to this than just staying alert and productive. Your brain needs a rest after a period of intense concentration, so it can ready itself for the next task or thought process. You can provide the right conditions to encourage your subconscious to produce solutions to your problems. If you believe you don't have time to rest, you probably need it even more!

Take full advantage of weekends to do the things you love. A two-day break gives you a real chance to rest your mind and body. When I was employed in local authorities, I regularly spent whole weekends working. Now I can see how stupid it was; I didn't give my brain time to recover from the demanding week I'd had. But it was hard to kick the habit because I thought I wouldn't be able to perform as well.

I don't want you to make the same mistake and realise when it's too late. It probably won't even be appreciated, and all you're doing is ramping up other people's expectations of how much you can do.

Life is for living, but it will also make you more effective at work in the long run.

Activity 25 - Set the conditions for flow

25.1 In your workbook, write about the following:
• What conditions will help you get into a flow state for longer periods?
• How could you create these conditions? Which techniques are you going to try?
• How will this make a difference to your productivity, i.e. both the quantity and quality of your work?
25.2 Set a trial period of at least a month, and test out your new techniques.
25.3 At the end of the trial, return to the workbook and make notes on what happened. Tweak and try again until you find what is best for you.

Key points

- Learn to cultivate a 'flow state' where the work feels effortless.
- Cal Newport's book 'Deep Work' highlights the problems caused by multi-tasking/attention-switching.
- Planning your day helps you create flow. Build in blocks of time for focused work and match tasks with your energy levels.
- Try tools to help you set the conditions for flow, such as the Pomodoro technique.
- 'Eat That Frog': do the worst thing first each day.
- Create downtime to ensure you are alert, and allow your brain to recover after periods of intense concentration.

13

TACKLE RESISTANCE

What is resistance?

Resistance is a force inside you which tries to stop you making progress. It likes the status quo, where it thinks you're comfortable, and it will give you lots of reasons not to change. It's related to self-sabotage; the sensation happens in the part of your brain which wants to distract you and pull you away from your task.

Resistance wants to drag you off to do something more interesting or relaxing. Personified, it's a devil sitting on your shoulder, waving at you and telling you to look in another direction instead. Writer Steven Pressfield (link) relates this to authors who struggle to be productive, but it's applicable to people in any walk of life.

Most of us have parts of the job we don't like doing. When we actively avoid them, they lurk at the corner of our brain, wittering on and demanding to be done, snatching some of our thinking time. Then we can't maintain our flow, and our concentration diminishes.

Resistance often pops up alongside fear. Your brain is primed to detect threats, a throwback to our cave-dwelling and woolly mammoth days, but it can't distinguish between a perceived threat and a real one. It doesn't realise the beliefs we tell ourselves are false. The more you resist, the bigger the problem becomes in your mind, until it seems far worse than it really is. Then you convince yourself you can't do it.

If you want to be professional and achieve your goals, you have to overcome resistance.

Procrastination

A common response to resistance is procrastination, the art of delaying things which you could easily and quickly do now. I've had to work hard to overcome it.

There can be a host of different reasons for avoiding a task, and we can be immensely creative at inventing more. Mostly it's down to discomfort. It can pop up as a feeling that something will be too time-consuming, a reluctance to try something we perceive as new or difficult, or a fear of failure. We are probably not engaged in it, or we believe it's boring. So we reach for something familiar and comforting to entertain ourselves.

The key words here are 'a feeling', 'perceive' and 'believe'. You're giving yourself false messages about your confidence in yourself and your ability to do a task. If you feel bad about delaying it, you may even believe you are useless or lazy. A deadline looms or passes and guilt is added to the mix. You then put even more pressure on yourself. This isn't helpful; it only makes the problem worse, because you feel even less like doing the task once you've attached all those horrible emotions to it.

The ironic thing is, every time I've gritted my teeth and done what I've been putting off for ages, it's been much easier than I expected, leaving me wondering why it took me so long to get around to it.

This is all due to cognitive dissonance. Your brain looks at the delayed task and struggles with the contradictory information you're giving it. Surely if it was so easy, you'd have done it? So it convinces you it must be big and scary. The longer it occupies your mind, the more it assumes elephant-sized proportions and clouds your judgement, switching off the creative part of your brain which is essential for finding solutions. The reality of the task is almost guaranteed to be much less significant than you imagine.

Activity 26 - Understanding procrastination

26.1 In your workbook, answer these questions to understand what procrastination means for you:
• What are you trying to avoid when you procrastinate?
• What has your procrastination cost you in the past?
• What will it cost you in the future if you don't tackle it?
• If the thing you're procrastinating over suddenly became easy, what would it mean for you, your colleagues, friends and/or family? What would you gain? How would it feel?

Beat resistance

Beating resistance is a matter of breaking the cycle of negative thoughts and emotions about aspects of your work and life. Strategies usually involve taking small steps to start doing the things you're avoiding, gradually building your confidence to a point where you consistently address unpleasant tasks earlier. This is all about doing what we know we must do, even when we're not motivated to do it.

Start by understanding why you need to beat resistance. If you don't break this cycle, you will put yourself under too much pressure, as your habit of putting things off grows. You always have to do the tasks eventually, so you end up rushing them, regretting not having started earlier. On the other hand, if you stop attaching negative emotions to tasks and just get on with them, you'll give your brain room to relax and come up with creative solutions.

Keeping your goals at the forefront of your practices and having a structure to your day, both of which I discuss at length in this book, are your best friends for beating resistance. But there are plenty of other approaches you can take, depending on your reasons for procrastinating.

If you are struggling to start something, ask yourself why. Is it self-doubt and fear of failure? Do you think you won't enjoy it, that it's unnecessary, or of low importance? Is it something new and unfamiliar which you're struggling to understand or to scope out in terms of the time and skills it needs?

I've created a five-point plan to explore these feelings: change the narrative, challenge the signals, prepare to do the work, do it, and celebrate. Here are the stages in more detail:

1. Change the narrative

Alter how you view the task. Where do your feelings lie on the Sumo Guy's scale of one to ten? How big is the task, in the overall scheme of things? Can you break it down into smaller steps? What's the longest amount of time it will take if you put your mind to it?

Reflect on previous successes and learning experiences: does it involve elements which you've mastered before, or can you recall a similar task you once procrastinated over, then did well?

Recognise the need to work with your natural skills and abilities; don't fight against them. Find relevant knowledge you can apply.

Try to anticipate the sense of achievement you will experience once you've put a tick against the task. Motivate yourself by imagining how good it will feel to move on to more enjoyable tasks.

2. Challenge the signals

If you feel resistance and start to procrastinate, question whether what you're doing now is more important than the task you're putting off. Don't confuse being busy with getting things done.

When you hear the ping of a notification, tell yourself you will look at it during your next break. If you touch your phone now, you'll be presented with another temptation to look at posts and messages.

If the distractions persist, acknowledge they are there, then take an active decision not to look at them. Eventually, you will recognise the resistance as the first part of the process, and it will become easier to progress to curiosity, interest and absorption in the task. It's natural; harness your awareness of this to overcome the difficulties.

3. Prepare to do the work

Create a 'Today' list using a single sticky note. Put the delayed task at the top of the list, with a realistic target you are certain to meet. Forget about the bigger To Do list for now.

Mix tasks you don't enjoy with those you do. Don't allow yourself to do only the things you feel like doing; you'll never get round to the rest. No one enjoys or excels at everything.

Time blocking is a superpower in the fight against resistance and procrastination. Set a defined slot for the task and put it in your calendar, then do only that at the appointed time. Make this a habit, and eventually you won't question it.

Give yourself a reward for doing it. The odd chocolate treat won't do any harm; just don't start looking for unpleasant tasks so you can binge on giant bars of the stuff! Knowing a reward sits at the end of the process will train your brain to do it in anticipation.

Try to find an 'accountability partner', a colleague or another SBP, and make a pact to spur each other on. Be accountable to each other and check in when you need to do a dreaded task. You could celebrate together, exchange tough love, or just provide mutual support and encouragement when things are hard.

4. Do the work

Just start the task, telling yourself you'll only spend fifteen minutes on it. You will soon realise it's nowhere near as bad as you thought, and carry on. At the very least you'll begin to understand the different elements of it, get an idea of how to go about it and estimate how long it will take.

If it's a massive 'frog', break it down into froglets (I know, it should be tadpoles, but that's not as catchy). Use small blocks and set ridiculously low targets for the amount of time or the progress you're going to make on it. I bet you will exceed them.

My biggest 'frog' is my accounts and self-assessment tax return. It may sound strange for an accountant to admit this. But I enjoy strategic work most, so I resent getting bogged down in the minutiae of receipts and invoices. I also know I'll need to make an on-account estimated payment for this year's tax liability to HMRC, which is a pretty big disincentive! So I do a small section at a time.

Another of my favourite tactics is to make sure the ugliest frogs are displayed on my monthly whiteboard, so they are staring at me every day until I give in and do them. If they are on the board, I know I'll complete them by the end of the month. I make sure my board is realistic and only includes essential goals, because it's a matter of pride to me to tick them all off before I wipe off the list and start to record next month's. If I've procrastinated about a task, it will probably be essential by this stage, i.e. both important and urgent.

If you are in a state of overwhelm and genuinely don't know where to start, find the smallest thing you can do. Taking one small step will make you feel better, and it will be easier to take another, then another.

5. Celebrate success

Beating resistance may be one of the hardest things to do, so you need to celebrate it. We don't celebrate enough, do we? How much time do you spend beating yourself up over what you haven't done, while failing to acknowledge everything you have completed?

I hope you have a display of Thank You notes on your noticeboard, to remind you how much you are appreciated by others. But there are other ways to make sure you value yourself just as much.

How about creating a success jar? At the end of a week, look back and see what you've achieved. Then write each success on a scrap of paper and put it in a jar. It doesn't matter how big or small your success is. Over time the jar will fill up as a visual reminder of the positive things you're doing. On occasions when you feel like you're wading through treacle, that you're undervalued or not getting much done, dip your hand in the jar and pull a few pieces out to read. It should help to motivate you.

I record all my achievements for the day in my diary. An alternative is a 'Ta Dah' list, which you can embellish with celebratory stickers or doodles, if that's your thing. There's a useful article (link) which explains the psychology behind it.

I love the idea of a Ta Dah list; it's a simple but effective way of celebrating successes. When your brain is in a positive state, it's much more productive. The article above says: "Unfinished items that we've left hanging are like cognitive itches" and 'That's why the end of the day can leave us with that nagging feeling that we couldn't possibly have been productive, given how much still remains to be done.'

There's no doubt about it; beating resistance will enable you to get more done. It creates positivity, which will help to break the negative feedback loop and make you much more motivated.

Activity 27 - Plan to beat resistance

27.1 In your workbook, list the most significant examples of work you regularly resist.

27.2 For each one, consider the headings in this section and note down any strategies you believe would be effective in making you do the tasks sooner.

27.3 If you struggle, refer back to your writing for activity 26 on the impact of procrastination, to remind yourself of why you need to address the delayed tasks.

Key points

- Resistance is a force inside you which tries to stop you making progress; it wants to keep the status quo.
- A common response to resistance is procrastination, the art of delaying things which you could easily do now. It often involves giving yourself false messages about your ability to do a task, and your reluctance to do it grows the longer you put it off.
- Learn to recognise resistance and procrastination by following my five-point plan: develop strategies to change the narrative you tell yourself, challenge the signals, prepare to do the work, do it and celebrate your successes.

14

BUILD CAPACITY

A word about context

One of the most challenging aspects of being productive as a school business professional is the breadth of the role, considering your limited capacity as a single employee. No matter how efficient you are, it's unlikely you'll be able to do everything that's asked of you. This is why it's so important to choose your goals and decide which actions will help you achieve them, to give yourself a fair chance of success across the full range of your responsibilities.

The size of your school can have a significant impact on your workload, in various ways. There will be fixed tasks which you have to do, no matter how big or small your school or trust is. These include budget preparation and monitoring, closure of accounts, responding to audit findings, statutory returns, reviewing policies, and regular reports to governors. There will be some variations in these, relating to salaries and departmental budgets, for example, but most fixed tasks involve similar processes.

Other areas tend to vary more with the size of school. Procurement is an obvious example, where a large school or trust may more easily go above tendering thresholds. Other examples are income generation, overseeing building projects, and liaison with payroll and HR advisers, where a bigger staff complement or being in trusts and partnerships can create more issues. I'm sure you can think of others.

Wherever you are on the size spectrum, there will be differences in how business management functions are carried out. The organisational structure, knowledge and skills and the way they are applied to the workload will all vary. Everyone is under so much pressure that it's hard to find time to take a step back and assess whether the right people are being asked to do the right things, or whether duties are spread fairly. So an imbalance can occur without you noticing.

A small school is less likely to have teams to share the load, and as an SBP, you may end up doing routine administrative tasks which would be carried out by lower level staff in a large school. This can be frustrating, because they keep the place ticking over, and often need to be given priority over your goal-oriented tasks.

This chapter is about building capacity and finding support. My points above mean that the suggestions I make may be easier for some of you to adopt than for others. As always, I encourage you to take account of your own context. But if you don't have a team, don't assume delegation is off the agenda. You'll see what I mean when you read on. Try to think creatively and don't be afraid to ask for help.

Business planning

By now, it shouldn't come as a surprise that I advocate forward planning as a way of addressing your capacity issues. You have a school improvement or development plan (SIP/SDP), but do you have a school business plan for the areas which come under your remit? I recommend it, especially if you are responsible for teams.

A business plan creates a focus, ensures nothing is missed, and helps you organise your own and your team's workload in a way that is fair and effective. With proper timescales, allocated responsibilities, resources and performance measures, it's a transparent way of documenting how everything fits together, and it provides a reference point for all staff involved.

If you are the only one working on business management, the work elements of the existing planning document you've now created will do the job. If you lead one team or more, consider extending it into a business plan which everyone can refer to.

Once you have consulted your team(s) and agreed the content of a draft plan with responsibilities and timescales, you should check that the balance of work is right between individuals, based on their knowledge, skills and capabilities.

You'll be familiar with the principles of such a plan from your SDP, so I won't labour the point with a detailed explanation. If you're unsure, try to find other SBPs who are willing to share their templates for you to adapt. You could do this by joining my Facebook group based on this book (see 'Keep in Touch' at the end). But be sure to make it a dynamic document which you use to act and track success, not one that sits on the shelf.

Quick fix or stay fix

Stepping back to understand where processes are clunky can be very worthwhile. Can you identify areas where the same problems crop up over and over again, or questions you're asked so often that you can recite the answers in your sleep?

What's at the root of it? You will probably find a problem which hasn't been addressed. Firefighting is resource intensive and wasteful; this is called 'Quick Fix'. You can resolve the problem quickly, but you have to do it afresh every time (often displacing another important task), because you haven't addressed the underlying issue.

Your priority should be to review the relevant processes to prevent the problem occurring in the first place. This is called 'Stay Fix'. I first came across it years ago in a management course but I can't recall the source. Tackling the fundamental issue will bring longer-term efficiencies, reducing the demands on your time and energy.

In some cases, you can quickly spot that it's a sudden problem which is easy to sort out. My finance team once had an issue with the admin team suddenly asking for lots of copy orders. We investigated and discovered the admin team leader had changed their filing system, and the staff found it hard to navigate, so it was quicker for them to ask my team for the orders! We soon sorted it out.

In other instances, complicated interdependencies make it harder to identify the real issue.

Here are some questions you could ask to isolate the issue:

- Do staff have clear instructions, a procedures manual or system notes? Are they updated for changes?
- Are new staff given proper training, tailored to their role?
- Does everyone understand how they fit into the process, and what impact it has on others if they underperform?
- Is an issue around personal performance preventing staff from completing work efficiently and effectively? Do some individuals slow everything down?
- Is there a 'pinch point' in the process: a task which doesn't fit properly or builds in a delay? Is it down to information not being readily available, or an overdue review for part of the process? Let the team map out the full process. They should soon be able to identify what needs to change.
- Are staff unwilling to search for answers, stuck in a habit of asking you because it's easier?

If you think the best of people, you might not realise someone is being lazy. But it does happen, and you may need to have difficult conversations. Hopefully, it's more likely that staff lack self-confidence or are not properly trained, and they need your support. In the long run, promoting self-sufficiency among your team members will save you a lot of time and effort, which you can redirect to more productive work.

A simple example is the system for ordering goods. How often are orders charged to the wrong codes? This can play havoc with your budget monitoring reports. You'll waste time trying to find out why a heading is overspent, only to find out it's a coding error, which then needs to be corrected. If you provide clear guidance to budget holders with examples of how to code common items, your financial reports will be much more accurate.

The Stay Fix approach can be applied to other areas of decision-making besides how staff do their jobs. Here are a few examples; I'm sure you can identify many more.

- Do you take a preventative approach to managing every aspect of your premises? Do you have a maintenance programme to tackle small faults promptly, so they don't develop into an even bigger problem?
- What about IT equipment? Are updates installed so you have the latest version of software? When purchasing any new kit or systems, do you make sure the specification is fit for purpose and that it will be easy for your staff to operate? Cheaper systems requiring a lot of manual intervention can cost more in staff time than supposedly higher-cost alternatives.
- Do you build penalty clauses for underperformance into your service contracts? Do you receive and monitor relevant data, so you can invoke the penalties when performance falls below the specified levels?

Activity 28 - Stay Fix opportunities

28.1 Identify any problems which could be solved with a Stay Fix approach. For each one, what's the underlying issue you need to address?
28.2 Write down your thoughts about an initial set of steps you can take to achieve a long-term solution.

Effort to Reward Ratio

You've probably heard of the Pareto Principle, which says that 80% of your results come from 20% of the work you do. The key is in identifying the 20% which has the greatest impact, so you can direct your focus to it. It will mean deciding to say no to other things or doing them more quickly or in less detail. At first you might need to justify your decisions to others, but your results will speak for themselves.

Why would you put lots of effort into something if it wasn't effective? But you need a benchmark to measure it. I've come up with an 'Effort to Reward Ratio'. This isn't a detailed calculation; it's based on your instinct about the balance between the effort you put into an activity and the reward, for example saving money, generating income, or reducing the demands placed on you by people or processes. Develop your instinct to suit your context.

Think about the decisions you make each day, the processes you go through, and how you communicate with people. Are they all worthwhile? Or is your day swallowed up in detailed operational tasks which don't get you very far?

Assessing your Effort to Reward Ratios

If you've done a budget review, how did you select the areas to look at? Did you take into account the work involved for each area compared to the potential savings? Did you calculate the cost of changing systems and processes? If you stop using a system, for example, you might save a small subscription cost, but staff may have to spend a lot more time inputting or collating information manually, when they could have been doing more productive work.

Pay is the area of your budget with the biggest scope for savings, so you may not have much choice but to explore it. It's still worth considering the balance though. The monetary costs of reducing expenditure in this area are usually limited to redundancy and perhaps pension strain payments, but the effort rating is high: selecting staff for redundancy or reduced hours, handling appeals, renegotiating contracts, changing terms and conditions, protection arrangements and implementing redundancy or early retirement policies. Notice periods and protection entitlements also cause a delay in realising the savings. However, the reduction in expenditure soon mounts up when it covers a full year.

What about changing contracts for goods and services? Are the savings worth the lengthy negotiations for either early termination or reviewing terms, or the compromises and risks involved in collaboration? Can you be certain the savings will materialise?

It's easy to get so wrapped up in the details of a budget review that you fail to spot the hidden costs of achieving the savings. I'm not saying you shouldn't review some budgets; I'm merely advising you to prioritise review areas using your awareness of the Effort to Reward ratio for each of them. Look for quick wins to prove your worth.

Reflect on the way you carry out your daily tasks. Are you being efficient? I've already given examples: using dictation and a stream-lined approach to managing emails. Are your systems (IT and process-driven) set up to provide timely information with minimal effort? Is your office organised so everything you need is to hand?

Income generation is one area where knowing your Effort to Reward Ratio can definitely avoid wasted time and energy. The ideal is passive income, where an initial effort can bring in money with limited ongoing work. How about an online crowdfunding page or an alumni association (if you can find ex-pupils to run it)? You could install solar panels or wind turbines, but be sure you have the legal right to enter into an agreement and research all the risks.

Some funding bids are time-consuming to complete and have onerous conditions such as data collection and monitoring. Consider whether the returns are worth it before jumping in.

By focusing your attention on streamlining systems, you will not only be saving time, but you'll also be able to achieve consistency. This could mean you won't have to build in so much capacity to resolve problems which shouldn't have occurred in the first place.

.   .   .

Meetings

Do you attend any optional meetings? Examples might be briefings by the trust or local authority, or networking sessions. While they can offer the opportunity to keep informed, if you are hard-pressed, they may not seem worthwhile.

Do a clear out of any which aren't productive; you might have outgrown them. But before setting yourself adrift, consider the possible impact. You might not be so well-informed about developments, or you may miss opportunities to raise your profile, attract new funding or make new connections who might provide support. Are there other ways to achieve the same outcomes?

It's a balancing act, and if you listen to your instinct and think things through, you'll find what's right for you. It's about squeezing every drop of value from your time and using it wisely.

Home options

You can also streamline your home routines to reduce the effort you put in. Can you do things in a different way, to remove or reduce the frequency of some tasks?

What about household chores? If you have a partner and children, can they help more? Even from a young age, children can be persuaded to do small tasks like tidying up, if you catch them in the right mood (and offer a bribe). Partners…? I'd better not comment!

Depending on your financial commitments, you could hire a cleaner, or find someone to do your ironing, gardening or window cleaning. It can make a real difference to your time and energy, and you're also helping others in your community to earn a living.

It doesn't have to cost a fortune; you can choose the frequency. My cleaners don't do our spare bedrooms, as they're easy for me to clean relatively quickly. I use a franchise, because it is hard to find reliable independent cleaners in my area and the company has to find a replacement in cases of sickness or holidays.

Identify hidden talents

Productivity isn't only about you; it's also about how you relate to others. Don't underestimate your influence on your colleagues. You may not realise they may see you as a role model. Use your credibility to challenge others to stretch themselves and grow.

If done well, this will allow you to pass on some of your less important tasks to them. Guide them and monitor their progress, as you are still responsible, but they could provide significant extra capacity to the school.

We often make assumptions about colleagues, only picking up clues which lie on the surface. Not everyone is forthcoming about their abilities and hobbies outside school. Do you know what your staff can do? Their hidden skills might fit perfectly with a new project. They may have specialist knowledge to solve a problem, be able to produce creative ideas for projects, or have useful contacts who can help in practical ways.

Look beyond your staff. Members of pupils' families, friends and governors will have talents which can save you money or generate income. Some may have useful connections with businesses, voluntary organisations, local celebrities or the media, helping to attract sponsorship or publicise good news stories. Others may organise events, make items to sell at them, and run fundraising campaigns. If they have experience in creative and technical professions, they could do things for you on a cost-only basis such as photography, designing brochures and constructing or improving websites. Obviously, you'll need to make sure you have any risks covered with insurance.

Two examples come to mind from my experience. The first was a lady who'd returned to my local area and started coming to our church, just as we'd started a fundraising drive with a target of £200k to restore the stonework. Believe it or not, she had experience of Heritage Lottery bids and bagged us a substantial one! The second was when one of my team managers used his creative talents to transform a management development session into a memorable event which stimulated lots of ideas and action plans.

To unearth these hidden talents, think about how much you already know about your extended community. Do you have existing methods of communication to find out more, such as surveys and newsletters? Be creative and find out what's beneath the surface.

Self-service

Moving towards self-service for citizens has been an important part of local authorities' responses to the austerity cuts since 2010, which according to the Local Government Association have removed up to 60% of council funding (link). Wherever possible, residents are expected to find out information from council websites, or complete online forms for anything from requesting waste removal to applying for school admissions.

Self-service is a classic Stay Fix strategy, saving you and your staff significant time in the long run with some proactive work up front. I'm sure you will have already explored some aspects of it; many schools use systems to handle interactions with parents. Members of my productivity Facebook group kindly provided some examples:

- ParentPay to collect income from families;
- text messaging systems, e.g. to confirm pupil absences and send important information;
- online systems for school visits e.g. to book trips and complete permission forms;
- medical information apps, notifying parents of minor accidents and when medication is administered;
- Google Forms to collect information from parents for a wide range of purposes and to conduct surveys;
- Booking systems for parents' evenings;
- Apps to allow parents to update personal contact information while complying with GDPR.

Have you exploited self-service systems to the maximum?

. . .

Website information

A common cause of many enquiries is difficulty in accessing information. You can test out the effectiveness of your website by creating a hypothetical question or scenario and asking your friends and family to pretend they're a parent searching for some answers.

Here are some questions you might ask them about their experiences when visiting your site:

- Does the site map provide everything they're looking for?
- Are any areas missing which a parent would expect to see?
- Is the structure logical, and do the headings reflect the language they would use?
- Does the search function produce sensible results?
- How easy and quick is it to find the information?

It will be a lot quicker for someone to amend menus and content on your website than for your team to answer lots of repetitive enquiries. Their time will be freed up to do more meaningful and satisfying work, delegated by you, naturally!

Other opportunities for self-service

There are lots of opportunities for self-service in some of the functions related to LA or trust services, pupil services and staffing. These include HR transactions (overtime, travel claims), online learning systems, school libraries, cashless catering and drinks dispensers.

If you are considering changing any systems, especially those related to data, finance, staffing and premises, check if there's an opportunity to introduce self-service processes. Suppliers regularly introduce new features, but if you rarely change systems, you might not realise what they can offer.

Deploying technology for high-volume transactions is a great way to reduce the level of routine work in areas like payments or collating and analysing data. Talk to other SBPs and find out what they've used. As well as recommendations, ask for warnings about poor systems. I'm sure everyone is now an expert on the shortcomings of a certain FSM voucher system, over which you had little choice!

Activity 29 - Self-service opportunities

29.1 Review the self-service systems you currently operate and identify opportunities you haven't yet taken advantage of.
29.2 Find people to test parent-focused information on your website. Act on the feedback and discuss potential improvements with your website coordinator.
29.3 Check existing systems to see if you already have the facility to introduce new self-service processes.
29.4 Ask other SBPs in local or national networks for advice on what's been successful for them.
29.5 Prepare a cost-benefit analysis of the cost of a new system or additional module, compared to the savings in staff time and any other associated expenditure.
29.6 Assess the risks in your proposals, then discuss the options for change with your SLT.

Lead change

Building capacity is a critical issue in leading change. You will need others to play their part, so it's worth spending time getting it right. Otherwise you'll use up all your energy getting people back on board, and you'll be diverted from your vital work.

Recognise that you've had the benefit of more time to think about the proposals for change than others have. You'll have been developing different ideas, probably with a select group of people, before getting to this point. Your subconscious will have been mulling it over for ages by the time you go public with your plans.

But it's new to everyone else, and they need time to absorb it and understand what it means for them, especially their routines and their relationships with others. It's best not to rush this stage; start consulting as early as you reasonably can, to allow it to settle.

The way in which colleagues react will partly depend on their own attitude to change, but you can help things along by taking care over how you communicate with them.

The Golden Circle approach

Leadership expert Simon Sinek's TED talk 'Start with Why' (link) is currently very popular; it's a good resource for developing skills in communication and persuasion. It's part of what's known as the 'Golden Circle' approach, as explained in an article on the Leaderonomics website (link). The original concept comes from the private sector, but we can adapt it to change management in schools.

First, explain **why the change is needed**, in a way that makes sense to your audience. Most people need to be persuaded that something is necessary and worthwhile before they go along with it. Sad to say, experience often makes us cynical, so when we hear about a proposal for change, our antennae start twitching away, trying to decide whether we're being misled or taken advantage of.

The 'why' is about selling the reasons for the change: why it will be better than the old ways, or what makes a new system necessary. Make sure you answer the obvious 'what's in it for me' question, which is usually most people's first reaction. Listen to the language people use when posing questions and reflect it back to them in your explanations. Give meaningful examples wherever possible.

For the population to obey the government's call to stay at home to reduce the risk of Covid-19, the 'why' was a global pandemic, with the potential to cause massive loss of life.

Explain **how you're going to approach the change**; what system or process it will involve? You need to generate confidence that it's achievable. How long will it take to introduce? Will it be incremental or sudden? When do you expect to start seeing the benefits? Tailor the level of detail to the part they'll need to play.

Be clear about the behaviours you expect from everyone involved in the new approach. Show them how they can make a contribution and add value. Explain clearly and precisely what you want them to do, and how it will all build up to success. If they feel uncertain and only hear vague descriptions, they'll be more reluctant; we like clarity about what's expected of us.

For Covid-19, the 'how' was the roadmap, a national enforced lockdown and closure of many businesses and services.

Paint a picture of **what you want everyone to do,** so everyone can imagine their role in it. Make your descriptions clear and relevant.

The 'what' of Covid-19 was the requirement for us all to stay at home wherever possible and comply with social distancing.

You may be able to test out the changes with a small group of committed, willing people. Model the desired behaviours yourself. Seeing an example is far more persuasive than hearing a theory.

The reason for failure when introducing change is almost always poor communication. Some people think they ought to know every-thing, but this is not always the case. Within the boundaries you deem appropriate, discuss things as openly as you can, and make yourself available to discuss concerns in private if it helps. This might seem time-consuming, but it will be a fraction of the input needed to manage conflict if the change is handled badly.

Once the change is implemented, it needs to be embedded. Keep watching and monitoring progress, and praise those who cooperate and help to make it a success. It's all too easy to forget this when you are faced with a host of problems demanding your attention.

Try to catch small issues as soon as they emerge, otherwise they may grow into bigger problems and the flow of change will be inter-rupted. Show understanding and tact, and be supportive, but at the same time make sure you aren't accepting lame excuses from any (hopefully a minority) who are resistant to change as a matter of prin-ciple and are determined not to comply.

Activity 30 - Lessons from change

30.1 Reflect on a previous change you've led and do some writing in your workbook on the lessons you learned. You'll find some prompts in the workbook.

Key points

- To cover your broad responsibilities, you need to consider how to create extra capacity, but remember your context will influence how you can achieve this.
- Developing a business plan for your functional areas can be an effective communication and reference tool to manage and monitor progress. You can use the planning document you've already created as the starting point.
- Replace 'Quick Fix' inefficient repetition with 'Stay Fix' solutions to resolve underlying problems.
- Use an Effort to Reward Ratio approach to judge whether tasks are worth the time, effort and cost.
- Uncover hidden talents in staff, pupils, governors and the wider school community, to create extra capacity.
- Maximise self-service in as many areas as possible.
- Leading change brings opportunities to grow capacity by streamlining processes, so approach it carefully and get everyone on board through effective communication of the why, how and what. Clarity from the start will reduce the risk of time-consuming conflict and implementation problems.

15

HONE YOUR SKILLS

Assess your skills

Reviewing your areas of high skill and competence and identifying where you can improve will help you to direct your time effectively, which is essential for productivity. It's also valuable to know when it would be too much of a stretch to acquire a new skill. Why spend time struggling, if someone else can do it far better?

Your job description tells you what you should do, and the person specification covers the core competencies for your role. Your appraisal should focus on the skills you need for your current priorities. Are your skills up to date?

Consider the tasks in your schedule for the weeks and months ahead. Are they a good match for your knowledge, skills and experience, or have you been drawn into areas outside of your capabilities? Do you have spare capacity for the learning, and will it have a longer-term benefit? Does your schedule include one-off tasks you can allocate to others who already have the skills? Reserve your valuable time for the things you, and only you, can do well.

A wish to be productive in your current role isn't the only reason for honing your skills though. Earlier, you did some visioning about who you are and who you want to be, so you will have some ideas for your future career plans. Think ahead and seize every opportunity you can to develop skills which will further your chances of landing your next and subsequent jobs.

It can be challenging to stand back and make this analytical assessment of yourself. You might like to find an accountability partner and create a safe space to attempt an honest assessment of each other's skills. Include softer skills as well as the more practical type. You can find online assessment tools, although some are more suited to the corporate world.

Activity 31 - Assess your skills

31.1 Make an honest (re-)assessment of your aptitudes and skills. What are your strongest areas and training needs?
31.2 Read your reflections on 'Who do you want to be?' (Activity 10). Are there other areas you want to develop?
31.3 Group your training needs under priority goal headings and use them in your next appraisal.

Improve your skills

Here's a tough love section. All too often, I see SBPs ignore their own development then wish they'd taken a course or been more proactive in building or joining networks. Don't be a martyr; you have just as much right to professional development as any other member of staff in your school. Just because you have a heightened awareness of the financial challenges in your school, it doesn't mean you should be the one to make a personal sacrifice.

A course, conference or meeting might spark an idea or give you new information which could help you solve a sticky problem. You'll make contacts, some of whom could be invaluable at times when you need to talk to someone who fully understands the pressures you're under and can provide encouragement and practical solutions.

Do you agree? I hope so. Now we can move on to where you should put your focus for the best improvement.

We should pay attention to our strengths when deciding which skills to improve. Here's why: your capacity for development is highest for your areas of strength. It's where the biggest gains lie.

Recently, I heard about a study which compared the performance of two groups who undertook training in speed reading. The first group consisted of average readers; they started off with a score of 90 words a minute. The second group, with above average reading speeds, had a score of 350 words per minute. They all took the same speed reading class. The first group went from 90 to 150 wpm after the class, but the second group improved by much more, from 350 up to 3000 wpm. This proved that by applying time and attention to your strongest areas, you have more scope to multiply your capacity.

Conversely, it can take a lot of time and energy to boost your skills in an area that isn't a natural fit for your abilities. You need to change your brain chemistry, which is hard, so the amount of progress you will make can be limited. If you relate this to the Effort to Reward ratio, you'll see why it isn't a good use of your scarce resources.

There's another benefit in further enhancing your strengths: it's a more positive experience than struggling with more challenging areas. You'll be happier, more engaged and more likely to succeed. It's applicable across your team and school too; when everyone knows their strengths and makes good use of them, relationships are stronger and better results will follow.

I'm not saying you shouldn't improve areas you find hard; clearly, you'll have to try to some degree, if they're part of your role. Just limit the amount of effort you put in to stretch beyond what's strictly necessary. Working on a weaker area will only get you so far, and paddling against the current is more tiring than going with the flow.

Try to find others who are strong in your weaker areas, whether among existing staff or by bringing in specific expertise for a limited period to complete a project. Money may be tight, but fast tracking a project is worth the investment if it achieves net savings or generates more income than it costs. On the other hand, the Stay Fix solution is to achieve a complementary balance of strengths in a team, then you'll be less likely to need external support.

How can you improve?

There are lots of ways to develop your skills. But first a word of caution: don't try to master everything at once. Getting too far ahead of yourself can result in wasted effort.

When I started writing, I spent a lot of time finding out how indie publishing worked. This quickly opened out into learning all about book formatting, publishing platforms, launching, marketing and promotion, website creation, mailing lists, blogging, and advertising. I loved learning it all, but what I really needed to prioritise was writing a first draft. There was no need for the rest until I'd actually finished a book, and with such fast changes in technology, by the time I was ready to publish, many of the tools had changed.

I've found the art is in knowing enough to carry you through the stage you're at, plus a few next steps. Putting learning into action straight away will get you further and will bring you benefits sooner than acquiring new knowledge you don't need yet.

It's a lesson I still need to learn; I live in a permanent state of curiosity, and my passion for learning sometimes overrides my common sense!

Be creative about your development choices. Attending training courses in person can be expensive and time-consuming if they involve travelling or even staying overnight. It can be much more effective to shadow someone in your school, or to arrange a visit to a nearby school to see their systems and processes.

I always advise SBPs to go to their local authority's Schools Forum meetings as an observer, especially in the autumn term when the following year's budget strategy for schools is being debated. Anyone can attend; they are public meetings and the minutes and agenda papers have to be published on a public-facing website in advance of the Forum meeting. It will help you understand the strategic aspects of the school funding system as well as the decisions that directly affect how much money your school receives.

Coaching and mentoring can also be highly effective, but expensive if you have to source them externally. Do you have staff with this experience, or someone who has the aptitude and could take a qualification to equip them to do it internally?

Reading nonfiction books is a cheap option, especially ebooks, which are useful for snatching odd moments to read. The Kindle app allows you to highlight the text to create a note; you can download all your comments and email them to yourself for future reference. But many nonfiction readers prefer paperbacks.

Audiobooks are great to listen to when you're travelling, walking or doing household chores. However, it's hard to go back and find key points. Some authors offer a discount if you buy the ebook at the same time as the audiobook.

SlideShare (link) can be a good free source of learning, with slide decks on a wide range of topics. TED talks on leadership and personal development can be inspiring.

Many organisations offer online webinars and courses, some of which are free. I'm starting to create my own series of online courses on school funding and finance; details will appear on my website and in my monthly newsletter when they are ready.

It is entirely reasonable for you to purchase books, courses and webinars from the school training budget. Think about wider topics: leadership and management, risk management, project management and tools like Excel. You might find creative solutions in other industries; sometimes a different perspective can help you find exactly the right approach.

The question of skills is a personal one, largely dependent on your role and personal experience, so choose your sources and style of training carefully. Make sure any training is shared across the school where applicable, making it more cost effective and beneficial.

Convey your messages

Do you find it difficult to explain technical issues to non-specialists? Finance is a complex area and many people's eyes glaze over at the mere mention of it. But a significant part of the SBP role is to help others to understand how they can play a part in achieving value for money and keeping the budget on track. The challenge is to avoid it taking up too much of your time, while making staff more proficient so they don't rely on you as much.

Staff at all levels will need the benefit of your expertise as well as the senior leadership team and governors. The whole workforce has a shared responsibility to secure value for money, as paid employees. Even if they don't take spending decisions, they can use their time more efficiently to help the school's performance.

Some staff will have budget-holding responsibilities. Do they have the confidence and skills to carry them out? Do they receive regular reports with the right level of detail? Or can they generate reports themselves whenever they need them? Do they understand the financial information they're getting? Are they using the systems correctly, such as requisitioning, ordering, goods receipting, and allowing for commitments where the invoice hasn't yet been paid?

Your expertise isn't only helpful to those with financial responsibilities. By making all staff aware of the school's financial situation in general terms, and identifying where you need to reduce costs or increase income, you can encourage them to economise, or suggest ideas. Think about what they need to know; obviously it won't be appropriate for everyone to have access to sensitive information.

You can use generic information to shock or intrigue, such as how much a single lesson costs across the whole school, or what the fixed costs are per year before you even deliver any education. If you haven't calculated this, try it, and see for yourself how effective it can be in making people more aware of how they spend their time!

Consider how you communicate financial information to your audience. How do you capture and hold their attention? Do the reports make sense to people who aren't confident about finance? Do you manage to convey the information as simply as possible and in a style relevant to their level of understanding, perhaps with charts or diagrams like infographics, or a presentation rather than a report? Have you explained any acronyms or technical terms?

Leadership and management

My aim for this book was to focus on personal effectiveness, and let you tailor the suggestions to your own role, whether you are leading large teams, managing a few people, or handling business management functions alone. Writing it has been a difficult balancing act, because I'm aware my readers are in a wide variety of roles and have different levels of experience.

However, a lot of the strategies I suggest can be applied not only to the way you organise your own practices, but also to how you lead and manage others. This aspect of your role brings added complexities, because you're dealing with the outlook, motivation, and abilities of a range of people.

If you are offered a leadership or management role, you should be given opportunities to develop the skills you need. Too many people are promoted on the strength of their technical abilities but aren't given the support to deal with the wider issues in leading and managing others, so don't be afraid to ask.

Try to find your own style, suited to your context and the team(s) you lead. Look for ways to encourage your staff to work efficiently and effectively. Focus on creating a positive and supportive environment to give everyone the best chance of achieving more as a team.

Dealing with conflict can consume a lot of time, so it's better to adopt a proactive approach ('Stay Fix') and identify problems as soon as they emerge. Understanding how to deal with contentious issues and deteriorating relationships will help you resolve difficult situations, promote harmony and create a spirit of teamwork. You will benefit from further developing your softer skills.

Remember: tools such as policies and procedures can help you manage most situations. Don't struggle alone; seek support and make full use of any services you have purchased.

Key points

- Assessing your skills and finding areas to improve will help you direct your time effectively. Seize every development opportunity to further your ambitions.
- Don't sacrifice your own development just because you are aware of the school's budget pressures.
- You can make the greatest improvements in your areas of strength. Use a variety of learning methods and put your new knowledge and skills into action as soon as you can, rather than gathering knowledge you don't need yet.
- Review how you convey complex financial information to non-specialists. Use some basic cost information to help everyone be more conscious of how they spend their time, to secure value for money across the school.
- Consider the leadership and management aspects of your role, being proactive to avoid conflict. Use existing tools such as policies and procedures, and seek support from wherever you can.

PART V

TAKE ACTION

Take
action

Maximise

Organise

Set the foundations

We're nearly there; I hope you've found the first three stages of the pyramid rewarding and that you have lots of ideas. But nothing will change unless you put those ideas into practice. So the final part, although shorter, is crucial: taking action.

In this final stage, I advise you to check that the culture around you is right before you make a big effort to improve your productivity. Then we look at making the changes, and reflect on what we've learned. So, let's ready ourselves for the final part of the journey!

16

THE CULTURE AROUND YOU

Assess the culture

Culture is difficult to define, and changes can creep up on you unnoticed. I consider this relevant to productivity because if the culture of your school clashes with your beliefs and way of working, it may not be worth putting a lot of effort into becoming more productive there. You might need to consider a move.

The culture of an organisation isn't a tangible thing; it's how the people in it behave, the messages they send and their approach to relationships. Messages are not only voiced; they can be found in body language, in the gaps between conversations, in people's behaviour (especially when under pressure), and in the care and attention paid to those who are going through a tricky patch.

We often imagine culture as coming from the top, through the messages we hear from leaders, usually communicated overtly. But they can also be subliminal, unspoken and absorbed through observing the behaviour of our leaders: how they respond to challenges, emergencies and run-of-the-mill pressures. The true culture doesn't always live up to the stated vision!

What part do you play in setting the tone/culture in your school or trust? What impression and messages do you give? It's worth reflecting on this when carrying out your leadership role in any given situation.

Do staff in your school pull together when things are difficult, sharing the load and giving each other support and encouragement? Or does everyone try to maintain a stiff upper lip, afraid to admit they are struggling? There may be signals which suggest the reality below the surface is different.

But culture isn't always created from the top of an organisation, especially if the leadership isn't strong. Staff may play a part, for example by being reluctant to take decisions and referring them upwards. It shifts the responsibility away from the team and places it back on a manager's shoulders. Before long, no one is willing to take a decision; they have all retreated into their comfort zone.

This dependency can arise for various reasons. Team members may lack confidence or might not be properly trained. If your staff are in this position, it's relatively simple to deal with: find ways to boost their confidence, or arrange the necessary training. You might only need to reassure them that they have the responsibility and the authority to decide on the right course of action.

The worst-case scenario is where someone is perfectly capable, but actively avoids taking decisions, for an easy life. In chapter 10 I referred to it as 'putting the monkey on your back'. You can unwittingly encourage this crafty behaviour by giving up, heaving a sigh and taking the decision or doing the task. Don't fall into the trap; watch out for the monkey and refuse to take it.

Try to develop your instinct and recognise when others are making excessive demands on you. People don't expect to be challenged back and will usually realise they've gone too far if you explain politely why you can't comply with their request.

However, it isn't always team members who are at fault. I've known managers give an impression that they want to control everything. They may be completely unaware that those reporting to them are afraid to take their own decisions, believing they'll be criticised for trying. Soon they think they'll never be good enough, become dispirited, and avoid taking the initiative. It's worth checking to make sure you haven't unwittingly caused this behaviour!

Management can be like raising a family. Giving your children wings to fly off and make their own mistakes is one of the hardest things to do, but allowing someone the freedom to try and fail gives them greater opportunities for learning. You might eventually lose them to another school, but in the meantime, they will add value to your team and ease your load by willingly taking on new tasks.

Cultural compatibility

Being in the 'wrong' job or school can diminish your productivity. By wrong, I mean incompatible with your beliefs and needs. Perhaps you don't feel valued. Without recognition, we struggle to keep up the momentum and may even start to harbour a grudge. Your productivity will dip, and you may resent the way your job eats into your leisure time, especially if you spend ages on an evening trying to fathom out the latest government announcement.

Humans have two ears and one mouth, but don't always use them in this proportion. Do your colleagues and your SLT colleagues listen to you? Actively listen, I mean? Are your opinions valued? More to the point, are they acted upon? Can you say the same for yourself when the positions are reversed?

We have an innate sense of whether we are comfortable within a culture. It can start as a nagging discomfort, but you can't quite put your finger on the problem. Eventually you will figure it out, and then you need to decide what to do about it.

You have two options for resolving the issue: challenge it, and try to change it, or find somewhere which is a better fit for you. It could involve going to a different school or industry, or you could set up as a freelancer, depending on your skills and experience.

Be careful to do a lot of thinking before considering moving; the grass is not always greener on the other side of the fence. First, I recommend taking a mental step away from your job so you can see it from a different perspective. Use the distancing technique within the activities below to identify the problems, and consider talking to your manager to see what can be done to improve the situation. If he or she thinks you're considering leaving, I hope they will want to do whatever they can to help.

Activity 32 - Should I stay or go?

32.1 If you're not sure whether this is the job for you, do some free writing to try to understand your feelings about it. The workbook contains some prompts if you need them.

Challenge for change

You may find it hard to pin down the exact reasons why you're feeling uncomfortable about your working environment, but it's important to try, otherwise you might make the wrong decision about your future. Rushing off to find another job isn't necessarily the right option; you may be able to fix things and be happier where you are.

Here is an exercise to help you explore the options for achieving changes in your current school and decide if they are feasible, or whether you need to give serious thought to a career move.

Activity 33 - Scope for change

33.1 List the aspects of your role which you dislike but which could be improved in some way. Flag them as crucial, desirable or optional. Desirable means they would make a real difference, but you can put up with them if they can't be changed. Optional items are little niggles, nice to change but probably not worth the effort.

33.2 List the areas where you're highly productive or have the chance to be. Flag as crucial, desirable or optional.

33.3 Make a wish list of changes which would enable you to achieve maximum productivity. Flag them as before.

33.4 The list in 33.2 is your benchmark for what motivates you. Set this 'List 2' aside for now; you'll come back to it later.

33.5 Consider the 'crucial' elements to improve in lists 1 and 3. Write down ideas for change to help you stay in this job.

33.6 How easy or difficult will it be to implement each change? How long might it take, and are you willing to wait?

33.7 If your answers suggest it's worth a try, develop a plan to make the changes happen.

Making the changes

To plan the changes, ask yourself some questions, for example:

- Whose help do you need to make each change happen?
- How might they react? Can you count on them?
- If they are reluctant to help, what's the best approach to persuade them to give the support you need?
- How long will it realistically take to achieve the change?

If you are struggling to commit to the changes, remember these are the things you said were crucial. What will it feel like if you succeed? Will you sense a load lifting from your shoulders, a recapturing of the enjoyment you felt when you started the job? Consider whether the effort is worth it.

Give yourself a chance to make things right before you decide your current situation is not for you. It can be a big step to search for another job which meets your expectations, and you can't guarantee that you'll be any happier.

Change or walk away

If your responses to the previous activity suggest you can't stay and improve things, don't rush into any firm decisions yet. Step away from it for a while and come back to it later. You might see it from a different viewpoint. Perhaps you weren't at your best when you did it.

If the evidence you gathered is still telling you things aren't right and there's no prospect of making them better, consider the options open to you. Would any of them involve a longer commute? What are the financial prospects? Look back at Activity 33 and review List 2, the positive aspects. Would they still be present in a new situation, especially the crucial ones?

If you are considering moving to a different school, do you appreciate the difference context makes? First think about options such as primary or secondary phases, mainstream (with or without SEN units/resource bases) or special, and LA maintained or academy (single or multi-academy trust). What about levels of deprivation, rural or urban, faith school or non-denominational, PFI or non-PFI? The list goes on. All can demand slightly different skill sets, depending on your role.

Is it time for you to move up to a more senior role? What extra skills would you need? If you are considering a role in a different industry, what attracts you to it? Do you know enough about it?

If you like the sound of freelancing, you'll need a cushion of money to cover the initial set-up costs, like website hosting, IT equipment, good internet access, and travel and/or accommodation for any early assignments you do until you invoice the client. Can you cope with volatile income? How will your decisions impact on family members, especially any dependents, whether young or old?

I won't go any further with this topic, as I'm straying beyond the scope of this book. I just want you to be absolutely sure changing jobs is the right thing to do. You'll need to know what to look for in any new opportunity, and the activity set out in the previous section will help you pinpoint this. But don't forget to make sure your current positives can be sustained in the new role and environment.

Key points

- Consider how your school's culture has developed, and what part you might have played in helping to set the tone. Look for signs of an imbalance in decision-making and control, and encourage your staff to stretch themselves.
- If you feel a sense of discomfort, for example if the school's culture isn't compatible with your beliefs, consider whether you should challenge it and try to secure a change, or find somewhere better.
- Assess the true scope for change by identifying the crucial items you dislike but which could be improved, and a wish list of things to change in school which would improve your productivity. How long will it take to make the changes happen, and are you prepared to wait?
- Do you have supportive people around you to help you make changes? Give yourself a chance to make things right before deciding to walk away.
- If the changes don't appear achievable, don't rush into any decisions. Consider the options carefully and make sure you aren't jumping out of the frying pan into the fire.

17

MAKING THE CHANGES

Take your time

I hope that now you've worked your way through the book, you have a list of ideas to improve your productivity. But it's important to take good care of yourself as you tackle them. It's tempting to rush off and start implementing all your action points at once, but please don't!

First, step back and look at your list. Is it a fair representation of the areas you need to change? Go back to the notes you made about your starting point. Make sure you weren't hyper-critical of yourself, suggesting changes that weren't necessary. We always seem to see our shortcomings before recognising our talents.

Everyone is different, with a unique blend of skills and abilities. Don't throw out your existing good practices in your haste to improve. Identify the approaches that will help you cope and achieve, understand why they're effective, and build on them.

Can you group your ideas for improvement by theme? Do some of them involve making a change in your working environment, or the way you allocate your time? It's a good idea to draw them together and check none of them are in conflict with each other. You might even be able to remove some, if you spot an alternative way to address the same problem. Keep your plans as simple as possible.

Consider which changes will have the biggest impact for the least effort. You can tweak the Eisenhower matrix approach to use for this purpose; just change each axis to measure impact and effort instead of importance and urgency. When assessing how much effort is needed to implement each action, think about which people you might need to call on for support. Can you count on them?

Incremental changes

Now you have a better idea of the changes you want to make, work out how you can take an incremental approach. In the chapter on habits, I described how building up small changes and stacking them can be far more effective than trying to do too many things at once.

Look at how much time your top priority actions will take. A good place to start is choosing one which you believe will be relatively easy to do for a big impact.

If you enjoy free writing or journalling, write down some thoughts, for example describing the problem you're addressing and the difference creating a new habit or stopping an unhelpful one will make. There are spare pages in the back of your workbook for this purpose.

Now schedule your first action/project, gather the information and support you need, and put it into practice. Use a chart or calendar to mark off your progress and motivate yourself to continue.

When you're comfortable with this change and it's becoming second nature, you can introduce another. If you don't keep a regular journal, make notes at various intervals on your experiences. They will help to motivate you when you move on to other more challenging habits or actions.

Give each change a chance, but if it's honestly not working, then don't push it. Leave it and try another strategy; maybe now is not the right time for it. You can always come back to it.

Understand success

Try to figure out which actions are most successful and analyse how you're embedding the changes. Why are some things more effective than others? Write about the problems you encountered and how you tackled them. Brief notes will do, but try to use vivid verbs and adjectives, so your emotions jump off the page when you re-read them.

What will you do with the extra hours you free up? Use them to improve your quality of life. Make it a deliberate choice, not an accidental taking on of yet more tasks!

Watch out for any external influences which affect your productivity, and try to find ways of overcoming or harnessing them.

If you think something isn't working, check you're doing it properly, not half heartedly or inconsistently. If you're giving it your best shot but it isn't working for you, abandon it and try something else. The whole point is that the system you develop has to suit you.

Activity 34 - Your productivity action plan

34.1 Review your responses to each of the activities you've completed in your workbook and use them to make a list of the actions you need to take to improve your productivity.
34.2 Develop the actions into a plan with realistic timelines and success measures, making sure you prioritise those which will have the biggest impact. Don't do everything at once!
34.3 Celebrate! You have worked through a series of important questions about your personal and professional life, making a series of changes which will bring opportunities to grow and achieve even more. Give yourself a treat!

Key points

- Don't rush into implementing your actions to improve productivity. First, take a step back and make sure your list is a fair representation of what you want to change.
- Create your plan, setting realistic timescales. Group actions into themes to help you spot any duplication. Don't throw away your existing good practices.
- Start with high impact and low effort actions, and gradually layer others on top. Use free writing to record your feelings as you make progress.
- Identify why you are improving and how. Embed the changes and review your plan. Decide how to use the time you free up to improve your quality of life.

18

REFLECTIONS

A recap

We've covered a lot of ground in this book, because productivity is a broad issue. You will have done some deep thinking about your situation and the improvements you want to make. At times you may have resisted or felt disheartened; that is perfectly normal. But I hope you have also felt energised, in control, optimistic and determined, because the journey is just as important as the end point.

Let's do a recap using our pyramid model:

Take
action

Maximise

Organise

Set the foundations

In the Foundation stage, you're building a strong mindset, tuned in to achieving the things which matter most, paying attention to self-care, knowing yourself and choosing positive habits. I hope you can make real progress in these areas; getting the basics right will undoubtedly make the rest easier. A house built on sand will wobble and fall down at the slightest gust of wind.

The Organise stage is important because your future productivity will flow from the decisions you make here. It involves choosing the right goals and identifying which are the most important to take your dreams forward. You now know how to free up brain power, time, and energy. It will be easier to set boundaries so you can say 'No' more often without feeling uncomfortable, and you should be using some time management tips to help you achieve more in your day.

Continuing upwards, the Maximise stage includes enhanced techniques to get into a flow state so you can go deep for better quality in less time. You understand the best ways to tackle resistance and procrastination, and can build capacity, allowing you to prioritise your own important tasks instead of running around after everyone else first. I hope you've taken on board the message that you shouldn't sacrifice your own development. Keep learning and growing.

Finally, the pyramid is topped with Take Action. Before diving into making changes, check if you're in the right place, where the culture of your school is a good match for your beliefs and values. Weigh up any alternatives carefully and decide whether it's worth your while to make changes where you are. If it is, start to take action in small steps, building incrementally for lasting improvements. Be kind to yourself and don't become overwhelmed. Test things out and do what feels right for you.

My final suggestion is that once you have built your action plan to make the necessary changes, look back at the first few activities you completed in your workbook. Does your plan reflect the hopes and aspirations you had at the start of this journey? If not, is it because you've realised other things are important? It's a good idea to check your course now and again, like a sailor would, making adjustments as you go.

Throughout this book, I have emphasised that you shouldn't regard the advice as a blueprint, but rather as a pick and mix offering. You are an individual, and your needs, ambitions and world view will be different to everyone else's. You have a unique mix of experiences and talents, and you need to find your own solution, but I hope my suggestions have sparked lots of ideas for new things to try.

This whole approach will be a work in progress as you journey along your chosen path. I hope you'll revisit it throughout your career and adjust elements of your plans as needed. Change is the only constant, as they say, and many things can happen to alter your intentions and your style of implementation.

You are welcome to join my Facebook group, Productivity for School Business Professionals (link). It started as a place where I could consult SBPs on their main concerns, to make sure I covered them in this book. Now we're continuing as a place for discussion and support on productivity issues. I hope that if you join, you'll give advice as well as asking for it, to keep it a strong and supportive community.

Thank you for buying and reading this book; I am grateful you judged it worth spending your time on, because I know how hectic school life is, even at the best of times. I sincerely hope it has lived up to your expectations.

I wish you every success and happiness in your journey.

BIBLIOGRAPHY

Please go to https://schoolfinancialsuccess/psbp-links for clickable URLs to purchase any of the books I mention.

Deep Work: Cal Newport
The Power of Habit: Charles Duhigg
Smarter, Better, Faster: Charles Duhigg
The One Thing: Gary W. Keller and Jay Papasan
Getting Things Done: David Allen
Atomic Habits: James Clear
Productivity for Creative People: Mark McGuinness
Productivity for Authors: Joanna Penn
Boost Your Productivity and Achieve Your Goals: Matt Avery
Be The Gateway: Dan Blank
Time Management for Authors: Katie Forrest

KEEP IN TOUCH

May I ask a favour? If you have enjoyed reading this book, I would be very grateful if you could spare a moment to leave a review on the site where you purchased it. This increases the book's visibility, helping others in the SBP community to find it and benefit from the advice.

The best place to keep in touch and find out about my plans for other books in the School Financial Success Guides series is my website, at https://schoolfinancialsuccess.com. It's where you'll find my monthly blog and details of my books and online courses.

The first three books in the series are:
    School Budget Mastery: the basics and beyond
    Leading a School Budget Review
    Forecasting Your School's Funding

On the School Financial Success home page there's a red button which allows you to sign up for my free monthly newsletter. It contains a rundown of all the government announcements in the previous month relating to finance and funding in education and schools, with a brief explanation and links so you can read the original if you need more details. Why spend time trawling the web when I've done it for you?

You'll also get to hear about my future plans and any speaking engagements or webinars that I've been asked to deliver.

Here are my links for social media platforms, which you'll also find on the psbp-links page on my website:

• My Facebook page can be found at: https://www.facebook.com/SchoolFinancialSuccess/. If you 'Like' the page, it will help it to be more visible in your feed.

• The Productivity for School Business Professionals page is at https://www.facebook.com/groups/ProductivitySBPs/

• Twitter: https://twitter.com/juliecordiner

I hope you'll join the community discussions in any of these places.

ACKNOWLEDGEMENTS

The idea for this book emerged as I saw signs of overwhelm among school business professionals on Twitter. I wanted to help by sharing my experiences and learning, gained from many years of juggling weighty responsibilities with a private life.

The SBP Twitter community is an amazingly helpful and encouraging place to be. You all inspire me with your dedication, courage and hard work in the face of such substantial challenges. I hope this book helps in some way, whatever stage of your career you are at.

Many thanks to the SBP newsletter subscribers who joined the Facebook group linked to this book and provided feedback as I wrote the manuscript. At a very busy time, you commented on my posts and helped to shape the content, giving examples of current issues as well as tools and approaches that have worked for you personally.

Above all, I want to give a very special vote of thanks to my beta readers, for taking the time to read my draft manuscript and giving such detailed feedback in response to my questions. I was blown away by all your positive comments, and your perceptive and constructive suggestions have been invaluable. Thank you so much.

ABOUT THE AUTHOR

Julie Cordiner is a qualified accountant and independent consultant specialising in education funding and finance. She has over 30 years of experience in local authority education services, including ten years as an Assistant Director of Education.

Between 2007 and 2015 she represented the Association of Directors of Children's Services on the DfE's advisory group on school funding, while the National Funding Formula was in development.

In 2015, Julie became a freelance consultant, advising schools and local authorities on funding reform, strategic finance and value for money, and co-founded School Financial Success with Nikola Flint. She now runs it alone, and in 2020 will start to offer online courses.

As well as writing books and blogging on school funding and finance, Julie delivers webinars and speaks at national conferences. Helping schools give children every opportunity to live their best life is a long-held passion.

Julie and her husband have three children and three granddaughters, and they love to travel, under normal conditions! Favourite leisure pursuits include reading, knitting, sewing, singing and walking on her local beach. In February 2020, Julie published her first novel, 'A Borrowed Past', a historical saga under the pen name Juliette Lawson. She has learned many productivity techniques to support her varied career, and is delighted to share them in this book.

facebook.com/SchoolFinancialSuccess
twitter.com/@juliecordiner

www.ingramcontent.com/pod-product-compliance
Ingram Content Group UK Ltd.
Pitfield, Milton Keynes, MK11 3LW, UK
UKHW021344280325
5216UKWH00013B/85